Author
MIKE WILKINS

FOUR FORTY-FOUR

and other Bits & Pieces

Endorsements of FOUR FORTY-FOUR

Rev. Sunder Krishnan served as the Preaching Pastor of Rexdale Alliance Church (in Toronto), from 1980-2016, and became its Senior Pastor in 1996. He is the author of several books, including *The Conquest of Inner Space: Finding Peace in a Chaotic World*, *Loving God with All* and *Hijacked by Glory: From the Pew to the Nations*.

> "Outside of the Bible, good books have been my major source of wisdom when it comes to following Jesus in the daily, unspectacular and inescapable dimensions of life. These books have played the role of the proverbial "three square meals a day." But we humans are also inveterate "snackers"—hence the many guidelines for healthy snacking. However, the literary equivalents of the latter are hard to find—especially when it comes to the pursuit of God. Mike Wilkins' *Four Forty-Four and Other Bits and Pieces* fits the bill admirably—a most enjoyable and insightful companion to *Glory in the Face*."

Endorsements of FOUR FORTY-FOUR

Dr. Bruce W. Longenecker is Professor of Early Christianity and the Melton Chair of Religion at Baylor University (Texas). He is the author of a number of books, including *Thinking Through Paul* (Zondervan), *The Lost Letters of Pergamum* (Baker Academic) and *In Stone and Story: A Pompeian Introduction to the Roman Setting of Early Christianity* (Baker Academic).

> "Mike Wilkins has long been one of my few heroes in life. In this heroic and engaging book, Mike accesses the wisdom of his own heroes, processes it through his own vigorous engagement with life, and articulates it in fresh and refreshing ways for today. Enjoyable and challenging at the same time, his holistic reflections leave no area of life untouched. Be blessed: read this book of pragmatic theological wisdom."

Dr. Carolyn Weber is an award-winning author, speaker and professor. Her books include *Surprised by Oxford* (HarperCollins 2011) and *Holy is the Day* (IVP 2013).

> "With Wilkins' wisdom, wit and infectious joy, set your clock to God Time. Along with God's grace, Wilkins' bits and pieces help to make us whole. A refreshing re-set of a read!"

Four Forty-Four
Copyright © 2018 by Mike Wilkins

No part of this publication may be reproduced, distributed, or transmitted in any form or by any means, including photocopying, recording, or other electronic or mechanical methods, without the prior written permission of the author, except in the case of brief quotations embodied in critical reviews and certain other non-commercial uses permitted by copyright law.

UNLESS OTHERWISE NOTED, "Scripture quotations are from the ESV Bible (The Holy Bible, English Standard Version), copyright © 2001 by Crossway Bibles, a publishing ministry of Good News Publishers. Used by permission. All rights reserved."

tellwell

Tellwell Talent
www.tellwell.ca

ISBN
978-1-77370-976-5 (Paperback)
978-1-77370-977-2 (eBook)

DEDICATED

To my good brother in Christ and faithful friend
Ray Majoran,
who made the suggestion.

TABLE OF CONTENTS

FOREWORD..xi
INTRODUCTION..xiii

THE BITS

CHAPTER ONE: Four Bits about TIME WITH GOD.................3
   The 1st Bit: Four Forty-Four..3
   The 2nd Bit: Beating The Sheets...4
   The 3rd Bit: A Time, A Place And A Plan.....................................5
   The 4th Bit: Walking In Prayer...8

CHAPTER TWO: Seven Bits about REGENERATION
AND WHAT COMES NEXT...11
   The 5th Bit: That Old Man...11
   The 6th Bit: This New Heart..13
   The 7th Bit: The Renewable Mind...15
   The 8th Bit: Serving Somebody..18
   The 9th Bit: Memory Work...21
   The 10th Bit: Off-Putting..23
   The 11th Bit: The Difference...26

CHAPTER THREE: Four Bits about MARRIAGE......................29
   The 12th Bit: A Spiral Path..29

The 13th Bit: Love...32
The 14th Bit: Respect..33
The 15th Bit: Oppositeness 34

CHAPTER FOUR: EIGHTEEN PRACTICAL BITS 39
The 16th Bit: Life By Crucifixion 39
The 17th Bit: Defining Faith 40
The 18th Bit: Feeling Bad About Feeling Sad........42
The 19th Bit: What Never Happenened.................44
The 20th Bit: Seven Aspects of Discipleship 45
The 21st Bit: First Purposes 47
The 22nd Bit: Knowing You Know........................48
The 23rd Bit: Truth And Love 52
The 24th Bit: Mountain Climbing 53
The 25th Bit: He Laughs, He Rages 57
The 26th Bit: The Devil You Know 60
The 27th Bit: Time To Run 62
The 28th Bit: Becoming Something......................63
The 29th Bit: Body Bribing 64
The 30th Bit: Peacemaking 65
The 31st Bit: Deciding Principles..........................66
The 32nd Bit: "Mateo": Gifts God Gives 69
The 33rd Bit: Handlebars.......................................71

CHAPTER FIVE: ELEVEN CONTROVERSIAL BITS 73
The 34th Bit: The Son Of God's Faith...................73
The 35th Bit: What Gifts Prove.............................77
The 36th Bit: If I Should Die 78
The 37th Bit: Sabbath-Keeping 81
The 38th Bit: Foreknowing Those.........................84
The 39th Bit: All Things For Good.......................85
The 40th Bit: Explaining Misery...........................86
The 41st Bit: The Promised Life...........................88
The 42nd Bit: The Great Zap Theory....................89

The 43rd *Bit:* All Kinds Of People 94
The 44th *Bit:* That Full-Grown Man 97

THE PIECES

CHAPTER SIX: TWENTY-TWO OPINION PIECES 103
Piece #1: Why There Can't Not Be A Church 103
Piece #2: Emotional Surfer Dudes 105
Piece #3: With Or Without A Big Stick 107
Piece #4: No Waiting? 109
Piece #5: A Box Of Little Sticks 111
Piece #6: Hard To Believe 112
Piece #7: Fruitless Questions 114
Piece #8: Everything Connects 117
Piece #9: "Haven't You Already Read That?" 118
Piece #10: Explanations For A Death-Bed Conversion 119
Piece #11: Thanking Someone 121
Piece #12: Not Everyone Who Sounds Arrogant 122
Piece #13: Abolishing Hearts And Minds 123
Piece #14: Three Dead Men On Happiness 125
Piece #15: The Complicated Matter Of "Free Will" 126
Piece #16: Carefully, Not Quickly 129
Piece #17: Assuming Normal 130
Piece #18: Only In Christ 132
Piece #19: Biblical Divorce, And What Comes Next 134
Piece #20: Wild And Un-Tame Words 136
Piece #21: Forgiveness, Conditional And Otherwise 139
Piece #22: Born In A Coffee Shop 142

AFTERWORD 145
ACKNOWLEDGEMENTS from the author 147
ABOUT "GLORY IN THE FACE" by the author 149
ENDORSEMENTS OF "GLORY IN THE FACE" 150
ABOUT THE AUTHOR 153

FOREWORD

For seven years in the early nineteenth-century, Robert Murray M'Cheyne served as a minister of the Church of Scotland. Sadly, he died suddenly in 1843—of typhus—at the age of 29. His death, I'm quite sure, was as much of a loss to the kingdom of God as the death of 39-year-old German pastor Dietrich Bonhoeffer in 1945, and the death in 1956 of the 29-year-old American missionary Jim Elliott.

M'Cheyne's good friend, Andrew A. Bonar, also a Presbyterian minister, bundled up his sermon notes, his poetry, his essays, some letters he had written, his still-well-known daily Bible reading plan, and other bits and pieces of his powerful, seven-year ministry, and had the whole collection published under the title, "*The Memoir and Remains of the Reverend Robert Murray M'Cheyne.*"

When I was in my late twenties, and longing to be the pastor of "a church of my own," both that young man, and that compendium of the "bits and pieces" of his pastoral work, were greatly inspiring to me. In this, I was not alone. They have been just as inspiring for a vast multitude of readers—the great Charles H. Spurgeon being one of the first. Every page reflects M'Cheyne's holiness of mind and character, and his intense love for Jesus Christ. And there is a "sweeter-than-honey" savour to his delight in Christ. Difficult to describe, but impossible to miss. Furthermore, the Bible reading plan he created for his congregation is the one that Martyn Lloyd-Jones used for many years. I am one of the great multitude of Martyn Lloyd-Jones fans who learned of M'Cheyne through him.

But I always thought that "The Memoir and Remains" sounded like the book was about the journal and the corpse of M'Cheyne.

On the off-chance that when I die someone will think about collecting my "remains", I have compiled these bits and pieces of my personal life and pastoral ministry, to save that person the trouble.

Mike Wilkins
Spring, 2018

INTRODUCTION

One of my favourite English literature professors at Queen's University was once called out by a classmate of mine for being opinionated. The agitated student said, "But sir, this is just your opinion!" The professor matter-of-factly replied, "Of course it is my opinion. I am a professor. I am paid to profess my opinions of the literature I am teaching you."

As it turned out, I learned more from that professor than from many other "less opinionated" teachers. I did not always agree with his opinions, but they all very usefully helped me form my own.

Some years after graduation, I was similarly inspired by the great Martyn Lloyd-Jones, who wrote, in the preface to his fabulously helpful book "Preaching and Preachers":

> Some may object to my dogmatic assertions;
> but I do not apologize for them. Every preacher
> should believe strongly in his own method; and
> if I cannot persuade all of the rightness of mine,
> I can at least stimulate them to think and consider
> other possibilities.

And so, for all the years I was a Bible-teaching pastor, I always attempted to be similarly helpful by expressing my opinions about the meaning of passages of the Bible (especially controversial ones), and on current questions of the day which were relevant to the biblical texts we were considering, and on the specific disciplines of a whole-hearted Christian. In the same spirit, these 44 bits and 22 pieces of my life, my life work, and my understanding of many related matters, are here set down in print. My hope is that they will be helpful.

THE BITS

CHAPTER ONE:
Four Bits about TIME WITH GOD

The 1ˢᵗ Bit: **FOUR FORTY-FOUR**

For all the years I was pastoring a church, it seemed that whenever someone heard that I set my alarm clock for 4:44 a.m., I was asked, "Why?" Often, the question simply meant, "Why so early?" So I told them. I got up so early because of a few things I loved—and because of a few things I hated.

I loved running early in the morning, all by myself on quiet country roads. And I loved the sunrise. I loved running alone on a long country road as the sun first appeared. I loved early morning runs in each of the four seasons, even winter; all winter long, leaving the house in the dark, returning again "by the dawn's early light." (Running in the winter months of 1997, I noticed for a number of weeks, and marvelled at, Comet Hale-Bopp before I heard anything in the news about what it actually was. That wouldn't have happened if I had been sleeping in!)

But I especially loved running in the very first days of spring, with the return of migratory birds, and the first appearances of buds on the trees, and then the blossoms, and then actual leaves. I looked forward to those

3

mornings all winter long, and I hated to miss any of them when at last they arrived. So I got up very early.

At the same time, I loved to spend early morning time with God: reading, and reflecting on, and praying about, specific portions of the Bible. I loved how those times stirred my faith, and deepened my love for God. And I hated to be a man who slept in instead.

That's why I got up so early. Early enough for some time with God. Early enough for a good run. And that usually meant about two hours early. So for me, in those days of parenting and pastoring, that meant getting out of bed by 5:00 a.m. But of course, there was always a bathroom that needed visiting, and there was fresh coffee and nice mugs in the kitchen. So I set my alarm clock, and the coffee maker's timer, accordingly.

On the other hand, sometimes the question about 4:44 meant "Why *that* exact time?" Here, the answer is both personal and quirky. I have loved birds all of my life. All birds. Except for vultures, which are despicable. But other than vultures, I have always loved warm-blooded vertebrates with feathers, hard-shelled eggs, toothless beaks, four-chambered hearts, strong, light skeletons, and fast metabolisms.

I first got serious about consistent early rising in the summer of 1977, when I became a husband, and didn't want my wife to think I was a slob of a man who lacked the discipline to "beat the sheets." An alarm clock beside my bed, then, was an important piece of equipment. In 1977, my digital alarm clock had "4's" that looked like birds flying fast in an easterly direction. So 4:44 looked like three birds flying in formation toward the rising sun. Those birds looked organized! And they seemed determined to be getting somewhere, as I too, at 22, meant to be.

The 2nd Bit: BEATING THE SHEETS

"Beating the sheets" is the opposite of being beaten *by* them, which is important because, as everyone knows, your sheets, in league with your pillow, your mattress and your blankets, conspire against you. The challenge, then, is to get out of bed the very instant the alarm clock sounds. The very instant! It's like walking out on a dock, and diving into the lake the instant you arrive at the end. Postponing the dive never makes it easier. As I have come to understand the universe, I have come to see that beating the sheets is preferable to all other methods of getting out of bed.

Here's how I do it. The moment I hear the alarm, I put one foot on the floor, and I pull both arms out from under the sheets. This works! The sudden cooling of one of my feet and both of my arms instantly takes the fun out of being in bed, and it does the trick of breaking me free from the dreaded Enchantment of Coziness—and the deadly snare of the insidious "Snooze" button.

The 3rd Bit: A TIME, A PLACE AND A PLAN

"A *time*" means that the first order of business in developing a consistent and meaningful time alone with God is determining the specific time of day that will best work for you. For me, it has always been early in the morning. The very first thing in the morning, actually. Training for a fall marathon, rather than a spring marathon, meant that all my really long runs were in the summer months. In those days, my "time with God" was the second thing I did in the early morning, after my run, and right after my shower. The important rule, in the matter of a long run on a summer morning, is "the earlier, the better." So I left the house at 4:00 a.m., which of course meant resetting my alarm clock for 3:44. But generally, I have positioned my time with God as the first thing. Either way, becoming an expert at instantly responding to the alarm clock is important.

"A *place*" is my brown chair. But this chair of mine is so much more than brown. It swivels. It reclines. And it rocks—in the non-vernacular sense. My brown chair is amazingly comfortable, and easily the most expensive birthday gift my wife has ever given me. (So expensive, in fact, I insisted she give it to me again that same year for Christmas.) But it's all good. I now spend so many hours in my brown chair, not only for my time with God, but also for other reading, and for writing (on my laptop), and for very short naps, that I have never regretted how much money my wife spent on it. I mean, we've had car repairs that were more expensive.

My brown chair is positioned right in front of a window, which is nice, and right beside a bookshelf, which is important. On that bookshelf, I keep my Bible, several books written by my Dead Men, and my journal. In a mug close at hand is a pen I like, an ever-sharp pencil with which to mark up books, an eraser, and a short ruler for underlining. With every required thing immediately at hand, I can avoid the interruption, annoyance, and inconvenience of not being able to find a pen or a pencil that actually works.

"A *plan*" is important, because, without one, you are, technically speaking, a person without a plan. Here is the plan I have been following for a lot of years. Of course, it has changed over time, but not much.

1. Seated in my brown chair, a good cup of coffee at hand, I begin my time with God by writing in my journal the morning's date: the day of the week, the month and the day of the month, and the year of my life. I do this a little ceremonially, taking note that this particular day of my life is one of a finite (and to God a definite) number I have been given in this world.

2. I read something that one of my Dead Men (see the 21st Bit) wrote, very often but not always, the "Morning Reading" from Charles Spurgeon's devotional book *"Morning and Evening."* In my journal, I usually copy a key sentence or phrase that stands out to me that morning—and sometimes write a personal comment about the statement's relevance to my present circumstances and immediate challenges.

3. I read a Psalm: one a day, though if the psalm is long (e.g. Psalm 18, 78, 89, and, of course, Psalm 119), I read a portion of the psalm. I read right through the Book of Psalms from first to last, and then I once again start at the very beginning. Next, I read from the rest of the Old Testament, one specific book at a time, one page a day. I write another journal entry, based on whatever especially arrests my attention. Day by day, I read through to the end of that particular book. From there, I almost never choose to read the very next book. Instead, I choose whichever other book of the Old Testament most strikes my interest.

NOTE: Every fifth day, instead of reading from any other Old Testament book, I read a particular chapter of the Book of Proverbs. I determine which chapter by dividing the number of that day's psalm by five. (For example, on the days I read Psalm 5, and then later Psalm 100, and even later Psalm 150, I read Proverbs 1 and 20 and 30. By this plan, I read (almost) the entire Book of Proverbs over a period of 150 (or so) days.

4. Similarly, in the New Testament, I read my way through one of the 27 books, but at the more studious pace of half a page a day because of the more concentrated content of the New Testament. Then I again make a journal entry.

5. Usually, but not always, I then read a few pages from one of the books of another of my Dead Men. That means that most days, I read something from two of my Dead Men, to begin and to conclude.

And that's it: my *plan*, for my *time*, in my *place*. But what about prayer? In the days when I was healthy and running regularly, I got up from my brown chair, got appropriately dressed according to the outside temperature, and headed out for a run. While I was running, I prayed about each of that morning's readings, as well as for the specific topics of prayer that I had assigned to that day of the week. For details on the topics, see the next Bit.

Since I have become unhealthy—and no longer able to run—I get up from my brown chair and dress for a walk instead. During that walk, I do the same sort of praying. I take my journal with me (unless it's raining heavily). At some times of the year, I also take a flashlight. Having my journal with me ensures that I remember the notes I made in the brown chair.

The 4*th* Bit: WALKING IN PRAYER

The New Testament teaches us to walk in love [Ephesians 5:2], to walk in a manner worthy of the Lord [Colossians 1:10], to walk in Christ [Colossians 2:6], to walk in wisdom [Colossians 4:5], and to walk in the light [1 John 1:7]. So here is a bit about my happy habit of "walking in prayer."

I began walking in prayer in an organized way when I was a newlywed. I learned to love walking around a particular rectangular block in our Richmond Hill neighborhood. I always did my Bible reading beforehand. Then, checking the outside temperature (using something we called a thermometer), I got myself dressed appropriately, and I left the building.

For each of the four sides of the rectangle that I walked, I prayed about one specific topic:

- a) The first side of the block I devoted to <u>prayers of praise and thanksgiving</u>, focusing on my current circumstances and recent experiences, and on what I had just finished reading in the Bible.

- b) When I turned the corner, I changed the topic to pray for <u>my family</u>, beginning, of course, with my wife.

c) Then I took the next corner, and prayed for <u>friends, both near and far, and some missionaries we knew</u>.

d) On the fourth remaining side of the rectangle, I prayed "freestyle." Often there was something about the upcoming day to pray about, or some new or ongoing challenge I was thinking about. Some mornings, I prayed about our future hopes and dreams, ambitions and worries. (We had some of each.)

A very significant thing about my "walking in prayer" has always been that, for the entire event, I remained mentally alert. (Especially on cold, dark winter mornings!) Once I learned to "walk in prayer," I never went back to my former practice of "sitting in prayer," which so often led to "drowsing in prayer."

CHAPTER TWO:

Seven Bits about REGENERATION AND WHAT COMES NEXT

The 5th Bit: THAT OLD MAN

The apostle Paul used the term "old man" to identify a human being (of either gender) who has not been regenerated, or "born again" [1 Peter 1:3, John 3:3,8]. Many modern translations of the Bible (for example, the English Standard Version) translate the words "old man" as "old self."

> Colossians 3:9
> … you have put off the old self with its evil practices… "

Every genuine follower of Christ, before being regenerated, was that sort of "old man." The Old Testament prophets and the New Testament apostles were very detailed in their descriptions of the inner life of an "old man," especially of his heart and his mind. For example, Jeremiah wrote, in well-known words, that the heart is *"deceitful above all things,* and *desperately sick"* [Jeremiah 17:9][1]. Similarly, Paul explained, the mind is *"alienated and hostile"* to God [Colossians 1:21], and *"does not submit to God's law; indeed, it cannot"* [Romans 8:7]. So here are every "old man's" two deadliest problems: a deceitful, desperately sick heart, and an alienated, hostile, lawless mind.

No wonder, then, that the apostle Paul stated that unregenerated people live "*in the futility of their minds,*" being "*darkened in their understanding, alienated from the life of God because of the ignorance that is in them, due to their hardness of heart.*" No wonder that he concluded that they "*have become callous and have given themselves up to sensuality, greedy to practice every kind of impurity*" [Ephesians 4:17-19]. Such is the desperate plight of every "old man."

Writing to a man named Titus, who was leading a church on the island of Crete, Paul reflected on those Cretans', and his own, "old man" days.

> Titus 3:3
> We ourselves were once foolish, disobedient, led
> astray, slaves to various passions and pleasures,
> passing our days in malice and envy, hated by others
> and hating one another.

Just like every other human, Paul and Titus (his "true child in a common faith") had been in deep, serious, personal trouble with God. But then "the goodness and loving kindness of God our Saviour appeared..." [Titus 3:4].

---

1   The context of this verse reveals that Jeremiah was specifically referring to the heart of the people of the tribe of Judah, whose sin was "engraved on the tablet of their heart" with "a pen of iron; with a point of diamond." [Jeremiah 17:1] In this, they were not unique; they were like every other human being with an unregenerated heart.

Thanks to the mercy of our great God, the gospel truly is very good news. The apostle Paul summarized the effect of regeneration with these words: "Therefore, if anyone is in Christ, he is a new creation. The old has passed away; behold, the new has come" [2 Corinthians 5:17]. So every "new man" should be careful to note, and to understand and remember, what miracles were required to change an "old man" into a "new creation."

The 6th Bit: THIS NEW HEART

In a familiar incident in the Bible, Jesus told a man, "Truly, truly, I say to you, unless one is born again he cannot see the kingdom of God." To this, the man, whose name was Nicodemus, replied, "How can a man be born when he is old? Can he enter a second time into his mother's womb and be born?" [John 3:3,4] It would have been better for Nicodemus, I think, if he had asked, "Will you please explain to me the miracle of regeneration?"

One way to begin to understand this miracle is to say that God makes the great, permanent, life-altering change that we call "regeneration," or being born again, by establishing each of his people in a new covenant. This is what the Old Testament prophets explained. And what difference does this new covenant make? Basically, what is involved is a heart transplant. The prophet Ezekiel passed on this good news from the Lord to the people of Jerusalem:

> Ezekiel 16:60,62
> "… I will establish for you an everlasting covenant
> … I will establish my covenant with you, and you shall know that I am the LORD…"

Later, Ezekiel provided details.

> Ezekiel 36:24-28
> "… I will give you a new heart, and a new spirit

> I will put within you. And I will remove the heart of stone from your flesh and give you a heart of flesh. And I will put <u>my Spirit within you</u>, and cause you to walk in my statutes and be careful to obey my rules..."

Jeremiah, the prophet, had a similarly spectacular message from God to his people—his deceitful and sick-hearted people, his people of the alienated, hostile and lawless minds.

> Jeremiah 31:31-33
> Behold, the days are coming, declares the LORD, when I will make <u>a new covenant</u> with the house of Israel and the house of Judah, not like the covenant that I made with their fathers on the day when I took them by the hand to bring them out of the land of Egypt, my covenant that they broke, though I was their husband, declares the LORD. For this is <u>the covenant</u> that I will make with the house of Israel after those days, declares the LORD: <u>I will put my law within them, and I will write it on their hearts.</u> And I will be their God, and they shall be my people.

> Jeremiah 32:38-40
> And they shall be my people, and I will be their God. I will give them <u>one heart</u> and <u>one way</u>, that they may fear me forever, for their own good and the good of their children after them. I will make with them <u>an everlasting covenant</u>, that I will not turn away from doing good to them. And I will put <u>the fear of me</u> in their <u>hearts,</u> that they may not turn from me.

So yes, regeneration is basically a heart transplant.

These glorious Old Testament promises of God were given to his people with a view to the truth that, in the future, from the perspective of the Old Testament people, the death and resurrection of Jesus Christ would make into one church everyone who believes in Christ: both Jew and Gentile. So these monumentally important covenant promises of God apply to *all* followers of Jesus Christ (see Acts 11:18; Galatians 3:26-29; Ephesians 2:11-18; Colossians 2:9-15 and, for that matter, the entire Book of Hebrews.)

The 7th Bit: THE RENEWABLE MIND

When the apostle Paul wrote that "we have the mind of Christ" [1 Corinthians 2:16], he did not mean that Christians have—or can attain—the intelligence of Christ, or his knowledge, or his wisdom. Biblically speaking, the "mind of Christ" is the *mindset of Christ,* or the *mindedness of Christ,* or the *mental outlook of Christ.* It means the God-given capacity to think about God, and about life and the world and the things of the world, in the same way that Jesus did, and does.

No one will ever be as smart as Jesus. But when God's Spirit produces in a person, once-for-all, a miraculous "change of heart" (see the 6th Bit), that miracle has a permanent effect on the mind also. As the apostle Paul explained,

> 1 Corinthians 2:14
> The natural person [by which Paul means an "old man"] does not accept the things of the Spirit of God, for they are folly to him, and he is not able to understand them because they are spiritually discerned.

But to those to whom God has granted the capacity to accept and discern "the things of the Spirit of God," the apostle's instruction is to get to work on their minds' renewal.

> Romans 12:2
> Do not be conformed to this world, but be transformed by <u>the renewal of your mind</u>, that by testing you may discern what is the will of God, what is good and acceptable and perfect.

> Colossians 3:2
> <u>Set your minds</u> on things that are above, not on things that are on earth.

Psalm 119 (perhaps most known for being 176 verses long) has a great deal to tell us about the specific help required by serious worshippers and servants of God. What this long psalm demonstrates most emphatically is that, generally speaking, God provides this much needed help for our mindsets through his Word: his commandments, his law, his statutes, his precepts.

> Psalm 119:10,11,18,25-27,34
> With my whole heart I seek you; let me not wander from <u>your commandments.</u> I have stored up <u>your word</u> in my heart, that I might not sin against you… Open my eyes, that I may behold wondrous things out of <u>your law</u>… My soul clings to the dust; give me life according to <u>your word</u>! When I told of my ways, you answered me; teach me <u>your statutes</u>! Make me understand the way of <u>your precepts,</u> and I will meditate on your wondrous works. Give me understanding, that I may keep <u>your law</u> and observe it with my whole heart…

In summary, by being born again (or, regenerated), we receive "a new heart," meaning a new capacity to love the things that Christ loves, such as righteousness, and to hate the things that Christ hates, such as wickedness [Hebrews 1:9]. When we are "born again," we receive a new heart, but not a new mind. But God gives his people, regarding their minds, the capacity to be "transformed." Paul called this particular transformation a "renewal."

As Psalm 119 (and other Scriptures) makes plain, the definitive way for the mind to be renewed is by meditating on the Word of God.

> Psalm 1:1,2
> Blessed is the man who walks not in the counsel of the wicked, nor stands in the way of sinners, nor sits in the seat of scoffers; but his delight is in the law of the LORD, and on his law <u>he meditates day and night.</u>

For me, there is one particular "Bible discipline" that has been the most effective practice for developing the habit of meditating on God's Word (see the 9th Bit).

EXTRA READING: In my preaching and teaching days, I never did get around to explaining an idea that I have been thinking about for some years: that the mind is something like a chess board. And so the game begins. Our hearts, with all their loves and hatreds, often put a piece or two on the board, which means we sometimes think about the things we admire, or the things we disdain. Our "flesh," with all those desires and appetites and urges and cravings and impulses and itches, also place various pieces on the board, some of them very powerful, some of them very ugly. Our memories, too, can place a piece or two on the board. As in a game of chess, the various pieces of thought placed on the board have an impact on some of the other pieces. So we get thinking!

The Bible, obviously, is a rich source of pieces to be positioned on the chess board. At the same time, people (in real life, and in the news, and on TV), books, movies, music, blogs, podcasts and other Internet realities, are all able to place pieces on the black and white checkered board that is a human mind. And God the Holy Spirit is able to place pieces, as well.

The devil and his agents, it seems, also can—but only when God permits them to [1 Corinthians 10:13]. In the very worthwhile and entertaining book, "The Screwtape Letters," C.S. Lewis depicts an experienced tempter who strategically places certain suggestions into his "patient's" mind, always with some devilish outcome in mind.

The point of this EXTRA READING is that the mind games we sometimes find ourselves playing will be much more winnable, and our minds will be much more at peace, if we keep certain powerful pieces on the board all the time. And that points us to the subject of meditating on the Word of God "day and night." Certain Scripture verses (for example, 1 Corinthians 10:13), and some doctrinal principles (the five "Solas,"[2] for example), when they are strategically positioned "on the board," can greatly contribute to us having "the mind of Christ," and "setting" our minds on "the things that are above, where Christ is" [Colossians 3:1]. In other words, the Word of God is able to renew our minds, so that we "may discern what is the will of God, what is good and acceptable and perfect."

The 8th Bit: SERVING SOMEBODY

The "heart." The "mind." And then there is the "flesh." In the New Testament letters of both Peter and Paul, the "flesh" means the entire collection of our physical appetites and urges and cravings and impulses and itches, in other words, our entire physical human-ness. The big issue for every Christian in regard to his "flesh" is the question, "Who is the boss?" One great change that regeneration produces is the God-given power to decide who or what serves what or whom. Therefore, the Christian is either the master of his "flesh," or its slave! If the Christian is the boss, which is how things are supposed to be, then he is a steward, a manager working for God to look after his entire humanity, his own

---

[2] The five Solas are Latin phrases that summarize the major tenets of the Reformation. "Sola" means *alone*, or *only*. In English, these five points are "Scripture alone, grace alone, faith alone, Christ alone, to the glory of God alone."

"heart," his own "mind" (which together can be called his "soul"), as well as that problematic third thing, his "flesh."

So the apostle Peter wrote to the Jewish Christians who were scattered like "sojourners and exiles" throughout the Roman Empire [1 Peter 1:1; 2:11] saying:

> 1 Peter 4:1–5
> Since therefore Christ suffered in <u>the flesh</u>, arm yourselves with the same way of thinking, for whoever has suffered in <u>the flesh</u> has ceased from sin, so as to live for the rest of the time in <u>the flesh</u> no longer for human passions but for the will of God. For the time that is past suffices for doing what the Gentiles want to do, living in sensuality, passions, drunkenness, orgies, drinking parties, and lawless idolatry. With respect to this they are surprised when you do not join them in the same flood of debauchery, and they malign you; but they will give account to him who is ready to judge the living and the dead.

The apostle Paul stated plainly to "all those in Rome who are loved by God and called to be saints" [Romans 1:7] that a Christian can choose to control his flesh, so as not to be controlled by it. (Paul's use, in Romans 6:12 and Romans 8:11, of the phrase "your mortal body" is equivalent to his, and Peter's, general use of the term "flesh" in other parts of their letters.)

Romans 6:11-18
So you also must consider yourselves dead to sin and alive to God in Christ Jesus. Let not sin therefore reign in <u>your mortal body</u>, to make you obey its passions. Do not present your members[3] to sin as instruments for unrighteousness, but present yourselves to God as those who have been brought from death to life, and your members to God as instruments for righteousness. *For sin will have no dominion over you,* since you are not under law but under grace. What then? Are we to sin because we are not under law but under grace? By no means! Do you not know that if you present yourselves to anyone as obedient slaves, you are slaves of the one whom you obey, either of sin, which leads to death, or of obedience, which leads to righteousness? But thanks be to God, that you who were once slaves of sin have become <u>obedient from the heart</u> to the standard of teaching to which you were committed, and, having been set free from sin, have become <u>slaves of righteousness.</u>

---

3 Paul's use of the word "members" in this text is a reference to actual "body parts": limbs, organs, bones, muscles, tendons, glands—our entire collection of the "pieces" of our physical being. In Paul's time, that was the only thing the word "member" ever meant. Apparently, the apostle Paul was the first person ever to use the word metaphorically. He invented the metaphor to explain the implications of a church's participants being connected to one another in "the *body* of Christ" [e.g. 1 Corinthians 12:12-27]. To this day, people are borrowing the metaphor from the apostle Paul when they use the word "member" to refer to anyone connected to any sort of organization—in almost every case, I think, having no idea that they are speaking biblically!

Both "slavery to sin" and "slavery to God" (and "to righteousness," as Paul calls it in Romans 6) are volitional enslavements, that is, enslavements of the will, enslavements you volunteer for. In other words, when you are serving sin, you are doing so because you choose to. And if you are serving God, it's because God has given you, as a part of your "new heart," the desire, and the corresponding ability, to choose Jesus as your master. This was what Martin Luther, in the 16th century, wrote about in a book he entitled, "The Bondage of the Will." And, in the 20th century, this was what Bob Dylan was referring to when he sang, "You gotta serve somebody."

The 9th Bit: **MEMORY WORK**

When I was 18 years old, and a very new Christian, I attended a series of "workshops" in Kingston, Ontario. The workshops were presented by three men who were in town to scout out the Queen's University campus, as they were interested in establishing a "Navigator ministry" at Queen's. Anyone who knows what The Navigators are all about will not be surprised to read that those workshops emphasised the memorization of Bible verses.

I had memorized some Scripture years before, not in Sunday School but at Commonwealth Public School in Brockville! (It was 1964. The world was different in those days.)

I did not find the memory work difficult. Mrs. Thurston, my Grade 6 teacher (who seemed quite elderly to me then, but who was probably 50), selected a total of 81 verses for the entire class to memorize over the course of the school year. She included five complete Psalms, and four sections of the Sermon on the Mount.

Eight years later, The Navigators "got to me." It was the spring of 1972. I had not made any attempt to memorize Bible verses since Grade 6. And it had not occurred to me to get back to it in the six months since I had come to personal faith in Christ. But at these workshops, the men introduced me to a systematic way of memorizing Scripture that was called "The Topical Memory System." I was hooked from the very first verse (which is 2 Corinthians 5:17.) For many years after that that system remained for me my very effective method of "storing up God's word in my heart" [Psalm 119:11]. And so I have been recommending the TMS for decades. It is still in print (from Amazon, for example). To anyone who takes my suggestion to heart, I always offer two essential keys to success.

1. Follow <u>every</u> instruction in the book!

    Don't break step with the system in any way, even the tiniest little way. Follow the directions to the letter of the law. It is the method that makes the system work so well. For example, the instruction book insists you always memorize only two verses a week (actually, two verse cards, which is sometimes actually three or four verses in total). Of course, when you are just getting started, it is the most natural thing in the world to go for two verse cards a day, at least! But this would be like starting a marathon with a 100-metre dash. In doing so, you would be breaking one of the most essential rules, for the whole purpose of the Topical Memory System is to develop a systematic way to make memorizing Scripture a regular part of your life, which will happen, systematically, over 30 weeks!

2. Every week, meet with a friend and recite your verses to him.

    The system's method is to recite that week's two verses, as well as the other memorized verses you have reviewed that week. Why this rule? Because you will only ever be sure that you have actually memorized your verses ("word perfect," with references cited *fore 'n' aft*!) by proving it.

Now it is 45 years later. What has my lifelong habit of memorizing Bible verses done for me? Those memorized verses (many hundreds of them eventually) have been my evangelism and discipleship training, my Bible education, and the primary component in my writing of Bible studies, study guides, sermons, and other public addresses. The verses I memorized long ago, in Grade 6, and in the years of my young adulthood, have been my most useful counselling tool. And they have been the main element in any success I have had in "abiding in the Word," and "letting the Word of Christ dwell in me richly."

Seven years later, when I was working for a publisher of children's books, I chatted one day with one of the company's salesmen. He was of Dutch ancestry, and an active member of a Christian Reformed Church. I got a conversation going with him about my Scripture memorization habit. I thought he would be interested—perhaps even impressed. But with a certain Northern European directness, he told me that he was shocked to hear that I isolated verses from their context (as proven by my "verse pack"), and that I memorized those verses by themselves! He asked me how I thought any Bible verse could be properly understood out of its context. By that point in my life, I had been called out, deservedly, about a lot of things I had said and done, but I had never been called out for this!

In time, I came to appreciate my new friend's point of view. In fact, I adopted his approach, and began memorizing whole chapters, and even whole books, of the Bible, experiencing for myself how right that "Dutch Reformed" man was. It turns out that a deliberate consideration of a Scripture's context produces a clearer and deeper understanding of that verse!

The 10th Bit: OFF-PUTTING

How sad it is to see a "new creation," outfitted with a "new heart," a "renewable mind," and "dominion" over his "flesh," living as he did before he was regenerated, before he had been given the power to live as a new creation in Christ.

It is surely a great tragedy for a professed Christian to fail to live a consistently obedient life. The apostle Paul addressed this tragic possibility in his letter to the Christians in Ephesus. The 5th Bit considered the plight of that "old man;" those people who have not surrendered their lives to Christ, and who "have become callous and have given themselves up to sensuality, greedy to practice every kind of impurity" [Ephesians 4:17-19]. Those tragic people Paul contrasted to people who have "learned Christ."

> Ephesians 4:20-24
> But that is not the way you learned Christ!—assuming that you have heard about him and were taught in him, as the truth is in Jesus, to <u>put off</u> your old self (*literally,* your old man), which belongs to your former manner of life and is corrupt through deceitful desires, and to be renewed in the spirit of your minds, and to <u>put on</u> the new self (*literally,* the new man) created after the likeness of God in true righteousness and holiness.

"Learning Christ" is an expression Paul uses to summarize the experience of coming to understand how a regenerated person actually does live for Christ. God's further instruction, of course, is subsequently to get good at it. "Learning Christ" involves learning how to cease the life you lived as an "old man" (Paul called it *putting off the old man*), and learning how to live for Jesus consistently—a great change of life, for sure—but well within the God-given, God-powered ability of every "new creation." That miracle Paul refers to as *putting on the new man,* since it has been "created after the likeness of God in true righteousness and holiness." So a certain sort of <u>putting off</u> and a certain sort of <u>putting on</u> is always, and continually, involved in leaving behind the old way of life and wholeheartedly beginning the new life of a strong and healthy Christian.

Paul also used the term "putting" in his letter to the Christians living in Colosse:

> Colossians 3:5
> <u>Put to death</u> therefore what is earthly in you: sexual immorality, impurity, passion, evil desire, and covetousness, which is idolatry...

Here, Paul's direction to <u>put to death</u> five specific sins can sound like a mysterious, even mystical, experience, and the phrase has caused some earnest Christians some confusion. But it need not be confusing. As Paul moved on in the letter, he addressed another five sins, again using the "p-word" in verse 8, but with less metaphor—and without any mention of death.

> Colossians 3:8
> But now you must <u>put them all away</u>: anger, wrath, malice, slander, and obscene talk from your mouth.

And then in verse 9, as if to more certainly undo any confusion his metaphorical instructions might cause, in his reference to one more sin, he simply told them, Don't!

> Colossians 3:9
> <u>Do not</u> lie to one another, seeing that you have <u>put off</u> the old self with its practices and have <u>put on</u> the new self, which is being renewed in knowledge after the image of its creator.

The expository lectures preached by Dr. Martyn Lloyd-Jones (on Friday nights in the 1950's and 1960's at Westminster Chapel in London, England) revolutionized my understanding of the Book of Romans, and my own life with God, by teaching me that simply and wholeheartedly saying, "No" (to the sins of "the flesh," of "the mind," and of "the heart") is well within the power of a new creation in Christ, and is the effective, God-given method by which regenerated people escape from the tyranny of sin through the power of the Spirit of Jesus Christ.[4]

The 11ᵗʰ Bit: THE DIFFERENCE

THE DIFFERENCE THAT CHRIST MAKES

The old man
- His **heart** is hard, deceitful, desperately sick engraved with sin.
- His **mind** is futile, alienated, ignorant, hostile to God, hostile to God's law
- This **old man** is dead to God. *(It was sin that killed him!)* He is **a slave to sin,** and so **powerless to resist his flesh.**

The new man
- A **new heart:** the law of God written on it; the fear of God in it; the love of God poured into it.
- His **mind** is not new but it is **renewable!**
- This **new man** is alive to God. He's been freed from sin, is now dead to sin, is now **God's slave,** is now a slave to righteousness and so is **able to control his flesh.**

NOTE: Along with all the astounding benefits of becoming a "new man" in Christ, as depicted in the above illustration, the prophets and apostles had yet more good news. Along with a new heart, a renewable mind, and the freedoms and moral abilities that these gifts provide, the prophet Ezekiel added to the list of benefits "a new spirit," and God's Spirit dwelling within us!

> Ezekiel 36:26–27
> And I will give you a new heart, and <u>a new spirit I will put within you</u>. And I will remove the heart of stone from your flesh and give you a heart of flesh. <u>And I will put my Spirit within you</u>, and cause you to walk in my statutes and be careful to obey my rules.

---

4   Lloyd-Jones' lectures on Romans are still available in print, and as free audio recordings at mljtrust.com.

A "new spirit" being what it is, and God's Spirit being who he is, neither of those important gifts of God are depicted in the above illustration. Or it could be said that they are depicted, but, being invisible, appear not to be.

CHAPTER THREE:

Four Bits about MARRIAGE

The 12th Bit: A SPIRAL PATH

I have always been happy with the first line of a poem I wrote many years ago. For years, it was always my intention to recite this poem, in its entirety, at every wedding I performed. But there is a problem with this poem of mine. I have only written the first line.

My poem begins like this:

"A marriage flies a spiral path, toward heaven or toward hell."

I may not yet know how my poem ends, but I've always been clear about its theme. Marriage, according to the apostle Paul, is a beautiful, and spiritual, and holy, and simple thing—but not an easy thing. What makes it simple is that there are only two essential rules: exactly two rules because a marriage is comprised of exactly two people. What makes a marriage not an easy thing is the oppositeness of those two people. God's design for marriage requires two people of the opposite sex. So there are always at least a few problems.

The one essential rule for a husband is to love his wife, with a love that intentionally imitates Christ's love for his "bride," that is, his church. To imitate Christ, a husband is to love his wife sacrificially, as Paul plainly explained, in some detail, in Ephesians 5:25-31. If this one rule for all husbands were ever to be ceremonially depicted with a symbolic gesture, I nominate a hug—a warm, affectionate embrace, with the new husband's strong arms encircling his precious bride. In my long experience as a married man and a pastor, performing many marriage ceremonies, and conducting the pre-marriage instructional sessions, I have observed that women generally do not object to the suggestion of this gesture's symbolic meaning, or of the hug itself.

The one essential rule for a wife is to respect her husband. This is what we read in the 24th and the 33rd verse of Ephesians 5. The respect with which the wife is expected to respect her husband is to be specifically expressed in a wife's submission to him. It turns out that, in these modern times, that is a controversial concept. Far fewer are the general objections to a husband's sacrificial love for his wife, but a woman's voluntary submission to her husband is actually a similar sort of sacrifice. "Submission" is the English word for the actual Greek word used by the apostle Paul. It was a military term, referring to the subordination of a soldier to an officer.

(**WARNING:** I am now going to suggest the symbolic gesture I believe would be appropriate for a biblically-minded wife to use at their wedding to depict her commitment to her husband, and to the one rule of marriage God has given to her. But I am actually very doubtful if any woman will ever appreciate the symbol, not to mention including it in the wedding ceremony. Even the woman most sincerely respectful of her husband, and heartily open to, and approving of, her husband's symbolic hug, may object to my idea. In fact, a woman may think, at least regarding my ceremonial suggestion for her, that I certainly am some sort of anti-egalitarian, sexist pig. But I will try not to be deterred by that. And no one will be able to say that I proceeded without first posting an alert.)

All right then. If the one rule for all wives were to be ceremonially depicted with a symbolic gesture, my humble suggestion is that that gesture be a salute—a smart, snappy military salute.

In the event that any woman continues reading this Bit, or even this book, beyond this page, I take another moment to explain my thinking. As every military person, and every fan of war movies, knows, a smart, snappy salute is a gesture of respect. What might appeal to those people about a salute (it appeals to me) is that a salute is also a sign of subordination, which, as I have explained, is the specific meaning of the Greek word translated "submit" in Ephesians 5:22-24.

I think the problem with this ill-fated, imagined ceremonial use of a salute in a wedding service has something to do with the oppositeness of the sexes. Generally speaking, it is men, not women, who love the idea of being a soldier, of wearing a uniform, of hearing the battle plan, of saluting an officer, of preparing to attack, of being issued a rifle (with a bayonet)—or being issued a Spitfire. But there just might be more to the wife's contempt for the gesture than this difference. And this is all I have to say about that.

Here, to conclude with the big picture, is a summary of the two God-given biblical rules of marriage.

> Husband:
> Love sacrificially! → *as Christ loved the church*
>
> Wife:
> Respect submissively! → *as the church respects Christ*

The 13ᵗʰ Bit: LOVE

There are two main reasons why God specifically commands men to sacrificially love their wives. The first reason arises from <u>a husband's most strategic besetting sin.</u>

Speaking very generally about every husband in human history, a husband's imitation of the sacrificial love demonstrated by Jesus in his death is made challenging, and even unlikely, because of <u>every man's natural self-centredness.</u> It is genuinely difficult for a man to care for his wife sacrificially because of his overwhelming commitment to his own appetites and desires. (Not to mention his constant, complicating supply of testosterone.) From this arises the tendency of a man to think that his home is his castle—and that he is the head of the home, whereas the apostles never said that. What the apostle Paul actually did write is that the husband is the head of the wife, as Christ is the head of the church. The church, being the "body" of Christ, rightfully expects its "head" to watch out for it, protecting and providing for every part of it. So, Paul was explaining, a husband, being the "head" of his wife, is obligated to protect and provide for her in regard to every part of her life. That was what Paul meant about the husband's "headship." If men were naturally unselfish, they wouldn't need to be commanded by God to love their wives with Christlike love. But they aren't naturally unselfish, and so they do need to be commanded.

The second reason that a husband is commanded to love his wife is that, speaking very generally about every wife in the history of the world, there is nothing she desires from her husband as much as <u>to be loved: permanently and passionately and sacrificially.</u> It is <u>every wife's one surpassing desire</u> for her marriage.

These two reasons explain why it is so important to the functionality of a marriage that the husband obeys the one order he has received from God, through the apostle Paul. Loving his wife in a Christ-like way is very much a make-it-or-break-it issue regarding the functionality of the marriage, and on this point, it is the husband that does the making or the breaking.

The 14th Bit: RESPECT

There are two main reasons why God specifically commands wives to respect their husbands. The first reason arises from <u>a husband's one surpassing desire</u>. There is nothing that a husband desires more than that his wife respect him. Her authentic respect for him is what he longs for. Whatever else his wife might be able and willing to do for him, if she has no detectable respect for him, anything and everything she does do for him will seem to him a bit beside the point. In any sort of marriage, the wife's demonstrated respect will always improve the marriage. When a man's wife says to him, "That's a really good idea, dear," or "You are so good at this sort of thing," or "I just respect so much how trustworthy and wise you are," that man will be motivated to love his wife more sincerely and more deeply.

The second reason that a wife is commanded to respect her husband is that, speaking very generally about every wife in the history of marriage, <u>women don't naturally think that men are all that respectable</u>, whether considered in general, or on a husband-by-husband basis. Sadly, there is lots of evidence, up close and personal, to support this view. Speaking personally, as one male member of the human population, I know I can be difficult to respect. To write here only of the "things of the flesh," there are times that snoring occurs, and from time-to-time there is nose-blowing, ear-wax-removing, burping and, um, passing wind. And really, how's a lady supposed to look up to all of that? Beyond the "things of the flesh," there are the "things of his heart," the "things in his mind," and the things he says when he is angry, or cranky, or tired. Many are the ways a husband can decrease his wife's respect.

The thing is, a husband is not likely to become more respectable if his wife serves him hefty portions of sarcasm and insult. But a wife can probably see for herself that when she praises her husband, or compliments him in any way, he is motivated to give her more to work with. For example, if she tells her husband that she thinks both his snow shovel and his lawnmower are sexy, he'll probably take a whole new view of yard work. He might shovel snow or mow grass every day of the year. But such talk doesn't often come naturally to a wife. The fact is, if women were naturally respectful to men, they wouldn't need to be commanded to be. But they aren't naturally respectful, so they do need to be commanded.

Concerning that spiral path that marriage flies, a wise married couple will notice that if the husband makes a concentrated effort to love his wife sacrificially, even if only because he is under orders from God to do so—and to be as respectable a man as he knows how to be, both his efforts will motivate his wife to respect him more and more. On the other hand, if the husband makes no concentrated effort to love his wife sacrificially, and continues to be (in his wife's mind) unrespectable, he will actually motivate his wife to respect him less and less.

Similarly, if a wife makes a concentrated effort to show her husband a great amount of respect, even if only because she is under orders from God to do so—and to be as lovable to her husband as she knows how to be, both efforts will motivate her husband to love her more and more. On the other hand, if the wife makes no concentrated effort to respect her husband, and conducts herself in ways he considers unlovable, she will actually motivate her husband to love her less and less.

So a marriage flies a spiral path, toward heaven or toward hell.

The 15th Bit: OPPOSITENESS

Two members of the opposite sex do well, once they are married, to always remember that they *are* opposites; about sex, for example. But this understanding often doesn't come easily—and it tends to be forgotten quickly.

One member of the marriage has been male all his life (although in these strange days, the point is sometimes debated). Because he is a man, a husband has a particular, inherent way of understanding the sexual aspect of marriage.

Being a long-time husband myself, I am happy to represent my gender by explaining what we men think we understand. What we men think we understand is that the sexual part of a marriage is primarily <u>a physical appetite of great psychological importance</u>. To men, sex is obviously something physical, because bodies are involved. To men, sex is an appetite, in that it resembles the other physical appetites. When a man is hungry, he looks for food. When he is thirsty, he looks for a drink. When he is sleepy, he plans a nap. And when he is feeling, let us say, frisky, he expects a woman to be there for him, poetically speaking. And sex is, to a man, of great psychological importance, because the privilege of "having and holding" his wife (in many senses, but, for the moment, especially in the sense we are presently considering) is of great importance to the way he thinks about himself, and how favourably he rates his marriage.

As for the corresponding issue of what wives understand, I can't, of course, speak with the same authority, or from any experience. But I have been married for 40 years, and I was a pastor for most of those years, so I do have an opinion about a women's opposite view of this major marriage issue. To a woman, I think, the sexual part of marriage is <u>an emotional experience of great relational importance</u>. To a woman's mind, sex is most importantly an emotional thing, and not a physical one. Sex is intimate and personal and loaded with meaning. It cannot be expected to just happen by being scheduled on a calendar. And sex, to a woman, is of great relational importance, because a woman just won't feel loved, particularly "sacrificially" loved, if the man seems to be going through the motions because of how it physically feels to him. On the other hand, the woman will feel very close to him relationally if the whole episode works out the way she is hoping.

What do these different points of view mean to married people? They mean that the *oppositeness* of the two sexes must be purposefully kept in both their minds. Both people in the marriage need to avoid forgetting that when they are talking to each other about the sexual aspect of their marriage (if they ever do!), it only seems to them that they are talking about the same thing. But the husband is talking to his wife about a physical appetite of great psychological importance. The wife is talking to her husband about an emotional experience of great relational importance. So misunderstanding each other is just about the most predictable possibility of all. Only if both of them can really grasp, and keep on grasping, their oppositeness regarding this aspect of their married life, do they have a hope of making sense to each other.

The oppositeness of the sexual component of a marriage invariably leads to the issue of "quantity versus quality." The husband is much more likely to be concerned about quantity. (In his mind, it's a physical appetite. "We eat three times every day!" he might think to point out.) Oppositely, the wife is generally much more interested in the quality of this part of their marriage; the quality, of course, being deeply related to the sorts of emotions the sexual experience invokes, and the effect that this particular experience has on their relationship. It seems to me, knowing perhaps almost as much about women as I think I know, that women are generally of the opinion that one important strategy for increasing the quality of the experience is to decrease the quantity.

So what's a couple to do? Happily, God has given us the answer to this important question. Both husband and wife must diligently follow the one specific instruction God has given to each of them. For the wife must believe that she is loved, truly loved, by her husband! And the husband must believe that he is respected, sincerely respected, by his wife!

It is simple, but it's not easy! Being happily and securely and productively married is hard work. But the Lord himself invented marriage, and he can be "a very present help in times of trouble." So I always recommend that a husband and wife sincerely commit the whole challenge to God, and then, as the saying goes, carry on.

It is all quite simple. But understanding your spouse is less simple for a husband than for a wife. So it is the husbands who receive from God an extra marital commandment.

> 1 Peter 3:7
> Likewise, husbands, <u>live with your wives in an understanding way,</u> showing honor to the woman as the weaker vessel, since they are heirs with you of the grace of life, so that your prayers may not be hindered.

I hope here that women will not be offended by the implication in this text that women are complicated. That may, in fact, be true. But "complicated" is a relative term, and here the degree of "complicatedness" is in comparison to men, who all ought to be able to admit are—at least, when it comes to some areas of life—very simple creatures.

CHAPTER FOUR:
EIGHTEEN PRACTICAL BITS

The 16th Bit: **LIFE BY CRUCIFIXION**

What a shock it must have been for people to hear Jesus say, a long time before his own crucifixion, "If anyone would come after me, let him deny himself and take up his cross daily and follow me" [Luke 9:23]. Crucifixion was an unspeakably cruel way to execute a person, and an unspeakably shameful method as well. It was apparently invented by the Carthagians (the people living in the city of Carthage in North Africa). When the Romans learned of it, they added crucifixion to their standard methods of disgracing, torturing and executing a criminal, or other enemy of the state. But it was to be used only for non-citizens of Rome. And so it came to pass that "Jesus of Nazareth, King of the Jews" [John 19:19] was shamed and tortured and killed by crucifixion. In the years to come, many of the followers of Jesus were, too—even to the present day.

So then it must also have been a shock for the Christians of the province of Galatia to learn that the apostle Paul believed that belonging to Jesus involved a sort of self-crucifixion! Paul wrote that "… those who belong to Christ Jesus have crucified the flesh with its passions and desires" [Galatians 5:24].

What did he mean? Crucifying your own "flesh with its passions and desires" means that you must sometimes deal with yourself, particularly your physical self, in socially embarrassing ways; in painful ways; in ways that involve a certain sort of dying. We servants of Christ must live in a state of readiness to "put to death" any of our appetites, urges, cravings and impulses that stand in the way of our obedience to our Master's orders.

As always, Paul set a good example to his fellow-disciples. He wrote, "I discipline my body and keep it under control…" [1 Corinthians 9:27]. Translated more plainly, Paul was saying, "I *blacken the eye* of my body and I *drag it around as my slave*…" Here is more incentive to get good at dragging yourself out of bed every morning at the moment your alarm clock goes off! (see the 2nd Bit)

The 17th Bit: DEFINING FAITH

If you ask some experienced Christian—a pastor or a Bible study leader, for example—for a definition of faith, you will almost always be pointed to Hebrews 11:1, which says, "Now faith is the assurance of things hoped for, the conviction of things not seen." This is a Bible verse. What it says about faith is true. But I would say that it is not the definition of faith. It is a description of faith, which is a different thing.

So then how should we define faith? It is an important question, since we regularly talk about having faith in Christ, and putting our faith in Christ, and trying to have more faith. Here's what I have on that.

To define faith, we must recognize that faith is made of two component parts. The first part is trust, which is sometimes in itself thought of as a synonym of faith. People talk about "putting their trust" in God, and "entrusting themselves" to God. But without specifying how much trust is required, and without answering the question of what exactly we are trusting God about, we still do not have a definition of faith.

Early in my years of pastoring, inspired largely by the words of Jesus about "counting the cost" and "renouncing all" [Luke 14:25-33] (see the previous Bit), and also the words of James about faith by itself "without works" being dead [James 2:17], I began to define faith as "the desire and ability to trust and obey God." Over the years, my definition lost weight, shrinking from nine words to six words: "trusting God enough to obey him." But the points of the definition remained the same. What do we trust God for? The strength we need to obey Christ. How much trust do we need? Enough to run all the risks involved in living in obedience to Christ.

Why must obedience accompany our faith? Because the only sure-fire indication that we *do* trust God enough to obey him is actually obeying him. Any other sort of faith goes with what Dietrich Bonhoeffer called "cheap grace."[5] Bonhoeffer's message to the church of his day was that genuine faith demands "the cost of discipleship." And the Lord explained that the cost is denying ourselves, and taking up our cross daily, and following him [Luke 9:23].

Not many of us followers of Christ actually will be crucified because we believe in Jesus, but being willing to die (or live) in shame and pain is the Christian prerequisite. So faith in Christ is *trusting Christ enough to obey God*. It is required of every disciple to wait and see what degree of shame and pain and death our obedience to Christ demands, and to wait and see what great things God will do for us, and through us, as we live to trust and obey him.

---

5 "Cheap grace" is, in Bonhoeffer's vocabulary, the opposite of "costly grace." See Chapter 1 of his book *The Cost of Discipleship*. In fact, see the first two words of Chapter 1!

A RELATED NOTE: A question worth thinking about concerns the significance of faith. The question can be asked like this: What exactly is it about faith that makes it the one essential human requirement for a right and lasting relationship with God? Or, why is faith singled out, even above love, as the requirement for justification?[6] Why is faith the primary thing that the Lord and his apostles called for when engaged in their gospel work? [e.g. Matthew 9:2,22,29; Acts 16:31].[7]

The answer, I believe, is found in the nature of faith. Faith is an intense sort of trust. For this reason, it can be compared to the vows of marriage, by which a man and a woman attach, or bind, themselves to one another. Faith, similarly, binds us to God. Faith works like some sort of really effective glue, so that we who believe in God—who have faith in God—become, in a very real sense, one with God. Christ is explaining this when he speaks to his apostles about the true vine and the branches. The branches that have been, and continue to be, attached to the vine, are pictures of people who have believed in Jesus, and continue to do so. Christ says that they "abide" in him, and that he "abides" in them. [John 15:1-5]. That they do is explained by the bonding nature of this "soul glue" that is called "faith."

The 18th Bit: FEELING BAD ABOUT FEELING SAD

"Don't feel bad about feeling sad." This was something I once said, spontaneously, to a very sad person. She did have something substantial to be sad about. But as she explained the terrible details, I could see that

---

6 Paul's statement at the conclusion of 1 Corinthians 13 that "faith, hope and love abide, but the greatest of them is love" only seemingly contradicts the primary place of faith in justification. In that well-known chapter about love, the apostle is not dealing with the subject of justification.

7 In the Greek New Testament language, "believe" is the verb form of the noun "faith." In other words, to "believe in the Lord Jesus" IS to "have faith" in the Lord Jesus.

she was burdened by more than the substantial thing itself. She also felt bad—even guilty—about being so bothered by her sadness. She felt it was an indication of weakness, particularly the weakness of her faith. So I tried to be of some help to her. I knew her to be a person of faith in the Lord Jesus Christ. So I spoke to her of the purposes of God, and of the many plain statements throughout the Bible of the good intentions of God that are even built into the difficulties he calls us to experience.

> Psalm 119:68,71,75
> You are good and do good; teach me your statutes…
> It is good for me that <u>I was afflicted</u>, that I might learn your statutes…
> I know, O LORD, that your rules are righteous, and that in faithfulness <u>you have afflicted me.</u>
>
> 1 Peter 5:10
> And after you have <u>suffered</u> a little while, the God of all grace, who has called you to his eternal glory in Christ, will himself restore, confirm, strengthen, and establish you.

So I said to the burdened lady, "On the basis of what God says plainly in his Word, you can be assured that this horribly sad thing has come into your experience according to God's steadfast love, and his faithfulness, and his good purposes. Apparently, he means for you to be sad right now. So go ahead! Be sad! And don't feel bad about being sad. Just be sad! And then let's trust God to comfort you through this sad experience, and to personally 'restore, confirm, strengthen, and establish you.'"

So she did. And God did. I have said substantially the same thing to many other sad people. And similar words to some angry, some nervous and some frustrated people, as well. But not to all of them. If there is something the sad person *should* feel bad about, that is a whole different matter. Wrong-doings of all sorts need to be dealt with; sins require repentance and confession (and restitution, if at all possible). It is appropriate for a person to feel bad about doing wrong, and to continue to feel bad about it until the thing is biblically dealt with.

The 19th Bit: WHAT NEVER HAPPENENED

In the early months of my life as a pastor, I got to know some fellow pastors who seemed frazzled. At the risk of sounding more analytical than compassionate (which is probably true, but I am hoping it doesn't show), I spoke to these pastors to learn what I could about how they had arrived at such a troubled state of mind. I learned that it was very often "the people side" of the work that was wearing these pastors down.

What I observed is that a common cause of the frazzled minds was "rumour fatigue." To guard myself from that condition, I thought through—and then wrote out and posted beside my desk—four principles to keep in mind for the entire duration of my pastoral ministry, which by grace I managed to do:

> *Many things reported never really happened.*
> *Many things quoted were never really said.*
> *Many things said were not really meant.*
> *Many things meant were not meant very much.*

Remembering these four simple principles prevented me from developing the questionable habit of leaping up—dropping whatever I was doing—to do something about some apparent occurrence that had just been reported to someone.

Of course, being directed by these four principles meant running the obvious risk of doing nothing when, in fact, there was something that I really ought to have done. But in my experience, that was a very rare occurrence. Almost always, it was only a rumour—about something that never really happened.

The 20th Bit: SEVEN ASPECTS OF DISCIPLESHIP

Shortly after I was appointed the "Minister of Discipleship," and the leader of the "College & Career" group at the church in Toronto to which my wife and I belonged, two young men, both university students from the group, approached me with a request.

"You being the new Minister of Discipleship," they began, "we would like you to meet with us and teach us all of your discipleship stuff."

I was very interested in investing time in the lives of these two bright guys, so I gladly agreed. We arranged to meet regularly on their campus to discuss the practical component parts of the life of a disciple of Jesus Christ. Subsequently, I did some organizing of my random collection of discipleship principles. The result was this seven-point list, subsequently fleshed out with details.

1. *Understanding the Gospel* [Romans 3:21-24]

    - The necessity of, and the work of, the Spirit of God in "repentance toward God and faith in our Lord Jesus Christ" [Acts 20:21]
    - The meaning of "justification by grace through faith in hope" [Romans 5:1,2]

2. *Abiding in the Word* [John 8:31,32]

    - Daily Bible reading
    - Inductive Bible study
    - Memorizing Scripture (and while you are at it, memorizing the titles of the 66 books of the Bible, the 8 divisions of the Bible, the 10 Commandments, and the Beatitudes) (see the 9th Bit)
    - Meditating upon Scripture [Psalm 1:1,2]
    - Listening and hearing from God through a sermon [Romans 10:13-17]

3. *Praying in the Spirit* [Ephesians 6:18]

    - Private prayer as a daily routine
    - Participating in small group prayer
    - Using Scripture in prayer
    - Understanding how to use the Lord's Prayer

4. *Walking by the Spirit* [Galatians 5:16]

    - The practical application of Romans 6:1-13
    - The experiential differences produced by regeneration (see the 6th Bit)
    - Bearing the fruit of the Spirit (e.g. how to develop self-control) [Galatians 5:16-25]. The practical application of Galatians 5:16 & 25
    - The meaning of "the old man," "the new man," "the flesh," "dead to sin," and "alive to God" [Romans 6] (see Bits 5-11)
    - Resisting the devil [1 Peter 5:9] (see the 26th Bit)
    - Fleeing "youthful passions," and pursuing righteousness, faith, love and peace [2 Timothy 2:22] (see the 27th Bit)
    - Seeking God's forgiveness for specific sins [1 John 1:9]

5. *Growing in Assurance* [1 John 5:13]

    - How a person can know he has eternal life (see the 22nd Bit)
    - The practical application of 2 Peter 1:3-11
    - What it means to believe that Jesus is the Christ [1 John 2:22; 5:1]
    - Understanding Christ as the Prophet, the Priest, the King in Hebrews 1.

6. *Exercising Godly Authority* [e.g. Romans 13:1,2; 1 Peter 5:1-3; Ephesians 5:22-30; 6:1-4]

    - The absolute authority of Jesus Christ [Matthew 28:18]
    - The limited nature of all (other) human authority

- The biblical design of a household, and of a church
- Exercising authority and submission in a household, in a church, and in regard to civil governments

7. *Working the Gospel*

- How to explain the gospel [1 Peter 3:15]
- How the gospel is the "power of God" [Romans 1:16]
- How divine sovereignty relates to human responsibility in the work of evangelism
- Developing and maintaining good relationships with "outsiders" [Colossians 4:5]
- Establishing a new believer in these seven aspects of the life of a disciple [Colossians 2:6,7]
- Understanding the words "discipling the nations" [Matthew 28:18-20]

The 21st Bit: FIRST PURPOSES

All the years of my pastoral ministry, I sought inspiration and instruction from a "hand-picked" group of servants of God. I called them my FIVE DEAD MEN. The total fluctuated over the years, but the criterion remained the same. Most of these men were pastors, John Calvin, John Owen, John Flavel, Jonathan Edwards, Robert Murray M'Cheyne, Charles Spurgeon, Dietrich Bonhoeffer and Martyn Lloyd-Jones. But they were not all pastors. George Whitefield was an evangelist. G.K. Chesterton was a journalist. C.S. Lewis was an Oxford don, and then a professor at Cambridge.

I chose each one of these men for the inspiration, instruction and direction I received from their lives and their writings. So then how is it that some godly men who never were pastors were selected to be on this team? I call it "The Principle of First Purposes." It is a principle that has had all sorts of applications in my life.

A pastor's challenges are many, and require many skills and insights. Each of these mentors of mine made the list for at least one particular characteristic I wanted to imitate. For example, Chesterton was an apologist. I became aware of him because C.S. Lewis mentioned (in *Surprised by Joy*) that *The Everlasting Man* had played a pivotal role in his conversion to Christ. I added GKC to my list at a time when both my pastoral and personal life were directing my attention to evangelism.

The Principle of First Purposes teaches me that everyone, and everything, can be of some value to each of us. Even a bad man can serve as a good example of what not to do, or of what sort of man not to become. And a good man only needs to be outstanding in one aspect of his life to warrant some of our attention.

The 22ⁿᵈ Bit: KNOWING YOU KNOW

> 1 John 5:13
> I write these things to you who believe in the name of the Son of God, <u>that you may know</u> that you have eternal life.

This statement of John's is, I think, his one-sentence summary of the purpose of the New Testament book we call 1 John. The book raises the question, "How can a person know that he has been given the gift of eternal life?" To answer the question, the apostle John refers to "these (three) things."

Thing #1:

> 1 John 2:3-6
> And by this we know that <u>we have come to know him, if we keep his commandments</u>. Whoever says "I know him" but does not <u>keep his commandments</u> is a liar, and the truth is not in him, but whoever

> <u>keeps his word</u>, in him truly the love of God is perfected. By this we may know that we are in him: whoever says he abides in him ought to walk in the same way in which he walked.

In other words, we know that we do know Christ, and so have eternal life "in him," if "we keep his commandments." Does that mean that we cannot know our status until we attain complete obedience to the commandments of Christ? Of course not. It can't mean perfect obedience, because there is no one in the kingdom of God who is capable of that. (For this reason, John writes the first verse of the second chapter).

The apostle must have been referring, not to perfect obedience, but to consistent obedience. "Knowing you have eternal life" is a dynamic thing, like the knowledge you have of a good friend. In the case of being a friend of Jesus [John 15:14,15], our assurance that we are his people increases and decreases according to the fluctuations in the consistency of our obedience. So the first Thing by which we can know we have eternal life is *consistent obedience to Christ*. It is a thing John returns to throughout this letter [e.g. 1 John 3:4-10]

Thing #2:

> 1 John 2:9-11
> Whoever says he is in the light and hates his brother is still in darkness. <u>Whoever loves his brother abides in the light</u>, and in him there is no cause for stumbling. But whoever hates his brother is in the darkness and walks in the darkness, and does not know where he is going, because the darkness has blinded his eyes.

Here, John plainly stated the second way to know you have eternal life. John returned to this second thing in Chapter 4:7-10, where he made it clear that this love for a brother must specifically be the love of Christ. So the second Thing is *Christ-like love for other Christians.* We should notice here that loving each other the way Christ loves us is itself a commandment of Christ to us [John 13:34,35]. So the first two Things are closely connected.

Thing #3:

> 1 John 2:21-24
>
> I write to you, not because you do not know the truth, but because you know it, and because no lie is of the truth. Who is the liar but he who denies that Jesus is the Christ? This is the antichrist, he who denies the Father and the Son. No one who denies the Son has the Father. <u>Whoever confesses the Son has the Father</u> also. Let what you heard from the beginning abide in you. If what you heard from the beginning abides in you, then you too will abide in the Son and in the Father.

The third Thing is not about right living, but rather right believing—but of course there is a direct connection between what we believe and how we live. The details of this third Thing become clearer each time John returns to it [1 John 4:1-3; 4:14-16; 5:1]

Thing #3, then, is *"correct belief about Christ."* In other words, to grow in our assurance of salvation, or to know more and more certainly that we have indeed received eternal life through our faith in Christ, we must be more and more correct in what we believe about who, and what sort of Saviour, Jesus is. According to John, the two most important things to believe about Jesus are that he actually became a human being, with both a human body and a human spirit, and that he is the Christ, which means God's uniquely anointed prophet, priest and king. This third Thing becomes clearer when 1 John is compared to Hebrews 1:2, about

Jesus being the Prophet; Hebrews 1:3, about Jesus being the Priest; and Hebrews 1:8, about Jesus being the King.

So John writes "these things to you who believe in the name of the Son of God, that you may know that you have eternal life."

> Thing #1.
> CONSISTENT OBEDIENCE TO CHRIST
>
> Thing #2.
> CHRISTLIKE LOVE FOR OTHER CHRISTIANS
>
> Thing #3.
> CORRECT BELIEF ABOUT CHRIST

These things being so, it has been my practice—when asked that old controversial question, "Can a Christian lose his salvation?"—to answer: "Well no. But a Christian can certainly lose his *assurance* of salvation."

ENDNOTE: As the Israelites in the wilderness with Moses needed to collect manna almost every day (or to go hungry) [Exodus 16:14-21], we who believe in Jesus must continually gather up the evidence of our salvation, almost every day.

ANOTHER NOTE: Along with the whole of 1 John, the other classic New Testament text on the subject of "growing in assurance" is 2 Peter 1. John and Peter were both apostles of Jesus, in fact two of the three "inner circle" apostles (along with John's brother James). All three of them were present at the Lord's preaching of the "Sermon on the Mount," and so heard the proclamation of these words:

> Luke 6:43–46
> For no good tree bears bad fruit, nor again does
> a bad tree bear good fruit, for each tree is known by
> its own fruit. For figs are not gathered from thorn

bushes, nor are grapes picked from a bramble bush. The good person out of the good treasure of his heart produces good, and the evil person out of his evil treasure produces evil, for out of the abundance of the heart his mouth speaks. Why do you call me 'Lord, Lord,' and not do what I tell you?

It seems that both John and Peter, two of the three apostles closest to Jesus, understood the particular significance of the challenge of knowing how to know you have eternal life. So both of them, decades later, wrote up what they had learned in their letters to the young churches.

AND ANOTHER THING: If anyone thinks to ask why then did James not also have his own version of the same explanation, the Book of Acts explains how it came about that James didn't live long enough to do so.

> Acts 12:1–3
> About that time Herod the king laid violent hands on some who belonged to the church. <u>He killed James the brother of John with the sword</u>, and when he saw that it pleased the Jews, he proceeded to arrest Peter also. This was during the days of Unleavened Bread.

The 23rd Bit: TRUTH AND LOVE

In the apostle Paul's letter to the Christians in Ephesus, he writes of "speaking the truth in love" [Ephesians 4:15]. Obviously, Paul is giving the Ephesians worthwhile instruction. Interestingly, in the Greek New Testament, the word "truth" is the verb in this phrase, not the word "speak." Therefore, a more plain (but less English-sounding) translation is:

> Ephesians 4:15
> Rather, '*truthing*' in love, we are to grow up in every way into him who is the head, into Christ…

Paul's point, I think, is that the corporate maturity (see the 44th Bit) of any particular church demands truthfulness in more than just speaking. Members of a church of Christ must not only speak, but must also think, and decide, and serve truthfully with the love of Christ.

The 24th Bit: MOUNTAIN CLIMBING

The knowledge of God is like a mountain, great and vast and towering. So growing in the knowledge of God is like climbing a mountain. The ascent is a great effort, with daunting challenges to be faced—challenges which intensify as the climbing continues.

Generally, the easiest parts of the ascent are the first parts. They are often much less steep than what waits above. And often, in the first parts, there are trees that provide shelter from the wind, with branches that a climber can hold on to. When the climber reaches the tree line, the challenges greatly intensify. More caution is needed, and more experience would be a great help.

But in the case of great mountains, a more serious impediment is still ahead. As you continue to ascend, the air molecules become increasingly dispersed. Breathing becomes increasingly difficult. To climb much higher will cause suffocation. Wise is the climber who knows when it is the time (and place) to stop trying to ascend. And so it is with those who pursue the knowledge of God.

> Isaiah 55:8,9
> For my thoughts are not your thoughts, neither are your ways my ways, declares the LORD. For as the heavens are higher than the earth, so are my

> ways higher than your ways and my thoughts than
> your thoughts.

Further complicating the climbing of the mountain of the knowledge of God, not all faces of the mountain are equally difficult. In our current times, the knowledge of God's love and mercy is easier to gain than the knowledge of God's vengeance and justice. In former times, the reverse was true. Similarly, the knowledge of God as a shepherd [Psalm 23:1] is easier for us to master than the knowledge of God as a consuming fire [Hebrews 12:29].

This is not to say that hard climbing is not worth the effort. For God says,

> Deuteronomy 4:29
> … you will seek the LORD your God and you will find him, if you search after him with all your heart and with all your soul.

So let us climb on! But let us be aware that—whatever face we attempt to ascend, and whatever height we strive to attain—there is always a limit to our ability to know and to understand completely the character, the ways and the thoughts of our great God.

> Deuteronomy 29:29
> The secret things belong to the LORD our God, but the things that are revealed belong to us and to our children forever, that we may do all the words of this law.

There is a very practical side to this analogy. A big part of this practicality is knowing which particular side of the mountain you should face, and then climb, and then take your stand upon, in your various personal circumstances. The side of the mountain we can call *the steadfast love of God* is a very good place to be when you're feeling alone, or afraid, or insignificant. But it is not so suitable a place to stand when you are being tempted to sin seriously. In those "dangerous times," the right place to stand is on the side of the mountain that signifies *God's discipline, and his justice, and his wrath.*

Every true lover of God should have some capacity to praise and adore and celebrate these "sterner" attributes of our holy God. Did you know that there are only four instances of the word "hallelujah" in the Book of Revelation? They all are found in Revelation 19, and three of the four are expressions of praise and adoration for God's "true and just" judgments and vengeance on the enemies of his servants. These enemies are metaphorically named "Babylon the great, mother of prostitutes and of earth's abominations" [Revelation 17:5].

> Revelation 19:1–4
> After this I heard what seemed to be the loud voice of a great multitude in heaven, crying out, "<u>Hallelujah!</u> Salvation and glory and power belong to our God, for <u>his judgments</u> are true and just, for he has <u>judged</u> the great prostitute who corrupted the earth with her immorality, and has <u>avenged</u> on her the blood of his servants." Once more they cried out, "<u>Hallelujah!</u> The smoke from her goes up forever and ever." And the twenty-four elders and the four living creatures fell down and worshiped God who was seated on the throne, saying, "Amen. <u>Hallelujah!</u>"

We do well to equip ourselves with specific texts that place us on one of the appropriate sides of the mountain most suitable to our circumstances. Consider these two contrasting sides of the apostle Paul's knowledge of God.

The first is, perhaps, just the text to reflect upon when invited to a social gathering that promises to feature specific, personally enticing opportunities to disobey God.

> Romans 2:4,5
> ... do you presume on the riches of his kindness and forbearance and patience, not knowing that God's kindness is meant to lead you to repentance? But because of your hard and impenitent heart <u>you are storing up wrath for yourself</u> on <u>the day of wrath</u> when <u>God's righteous judgment will be revealed.</u>

On the other hand, in our times of regret and repentance, for example, when we have come to our senses about what we now see was deliberate disobedience, this text might be just what the Divine Physician prescribes.

> Ephesians 2:1–10
> And you were dead in the trespasses and sins in which you once walked, following the course of this world, following the prince of the power of the air, the spirit that is now at work in the sons of disobedience—among whom we all once lived in the passions of our flesh, carrying out the desires of the body and the mind, and were <u>by nature children of wrath,</u> like the rest of mankind. But <u>God, being rich in mercy, because of the great love with which he loved us, even when we were dead in our trespasses, made us alive together with Christ—by grace you have been saved</u>—and raised us up with him and seated us with him in the heavenly places in Christ Jesus, so that in the coming ages he might show <u>the immeasurable riches of his grace in kindness toward us</u> in Christ Jesus. For by grace

> you have been saved through faith. And this is not your own doing; it is the gift of God, not a result of works, so that no one may boast. For <u>we are his workmanship</u>, created in Christ Jesus for good works, which God prepared beforehand, that we should walk in them.

The knowledge of God is like a mountain, great and vast and towering. No one can stand on every side of the mountain at the same time. Let us choose carefully the one side to stand on under our own present circumstances—at as great an elevation as we can.

> Proverbs 9:10
> The fear of the Lord is the beginning of wisdom,
> and the knowledge of the Holy One is insight.

The 25th Bit: **HE LAUGHS, HE RAGES**

A great help to me in my ambition to be a man without a temper was to learn the striking similarity between laughter and anger. Both have at their root the effect of incongruity, which can be pictured as the discovery that a square peg does not fit into a round hole, when all the time someone thought it would.

Laughter, on the one hand, is caused by an incongruity that surprises and amuses. This is the whole basis of a joke, which always ends in a punch line, which always contains an incongruity. For example,

> A pirate walks into a bar and says, "I've just come back from sailing the Eight Seas!"
>
> The bartender replies, "Don't you mean the Seven Seas?"

"Arrr!" says the pirate. "I thought that last one looked familiar!"

Maybe it's just me, but that particular punch line never ceases to amuse. (If you can't see why, feel free to "Ask the Author" on the website that goes with this book. 444book.com)

Anger, on the other hand, is caused by an incongruity that annoys, or offends, or injures. In every case, the annoyance or offense or injury involves an unmet expectation. We all have expectations and some of them are valid, which is why some anger is justified. A married person has an expectation that his or her spouse will be faithful "as long as we both shall live." That expectation is entirely justified because faithfulness had been mutually promised (before witnesses!) When a married person learns that adultery has been committed, anger is the right response.

But many expectations are not valid, and the anger it arouses is not justified. Allow me to illustrate…

The 1980's were a great decade for my wife and me. Our children were all born in that decade, and grew to be ten and seven and four years old by the time that decade was over. Predictably, the 1990's were more challenging for us as the children proceeded to become 20, 17 and 14 years old. For quite a while, I often started my weekday evenings at home by walking through our front door, taking off my shoes and opening the front hall closet. There I would invariably find that, contrary to my personal expectations, the shoes that the five members of the Wilkins family kept in that closet were not correctly paired, and not arranged in five distinct collections. In fact, some of the shoes were not inside the closet at all!

The result was that, for quite a while, for months that turned into years, I would, from time to time, begin my regular family evening with a display of anger that I am still embarrassed to recall. For example, rather than calling out a cheerful announcement that I was home,

I would ask a question, to no one in particular, in a loud voice. "WHY IS IT THAT A FAMILY OF INTELLIGENT PEOPLE CANNOT GRASP THE CONCEPT OF AN ORGANIZED CLOSET???" (Or something like that.)

This never turned out to be a good way to re-enter family life—and the result, I think, was that, from time to time, I was known in my own home as, among other things, a man with a temper.

Happily, and significantly, it eventually occurred to me that my expectation of a front hall closet organized with military precision was not reasonable. With that realization, I came to see that my anger was more than just a lousy way to start my evening at home. It was also unfair to both my wife and our kids, who during the homeschool years, were repeatedly in and out of the front door every day, all week long. So I repented of my selfish expectation, and asked the Lord for his help in demonstrating "the fruit of the Spirit," especially love, patience, kindness, gentleness and self-control [Galatians 5:22,23]. I learned that deliberately praying for myself and my attitude before I walked through the front door was a great help, for God is "a very present help in time of trouble," even stupid trouble.

Understanding that anger and laughter are cousins, I learned to be amused at my own unreasonableness. And so, at least as far as the front hall closet and the large pile of shoes and boots were concerned, we all lived happily ever after.

The 26th Bit: THE DEVIL YOU KNOW

In his introduction to *The Screwtape Letters,* C.S. Lewis writes:

> There are two equal and opposite errors into which our race can fall about the devils. One is to disbelieve in their existence. The other is to believe, and to feel an excessive and unhealthy interest in them.

So then, striving to avoid both of these errors, what is a person to do? The first thing is to believe in the existence of the devil (and his cohorts).

> 1 Peter 5:8
> Be sober-minded; be watchful. <u>Your adversary the devil</u> prowls around like a roaring lion, seeking someone to devour.

To deny the existence of the devil (and company) is to assist them in their destructive intentions.

The second thing to do is to "resist" the devil.

> 1 Peter 5:9
> Resist him, firm in your faith, knowing that the same kinds of suffering are being experienced by your brotherhood throughout the world.

There are some things we are told to "flee," as serious followers of Christ (see the 27th Bit), but we are *not* instructed to flee the devil.

What does resisting the devil mean? It means that immediately upon recognizing, or perhaps just having a hunch, that some thought is the work of the devil—or some series of evil thoughts, or some specific temptations—you must stir up your heart and set your mind to the urgent task of refusing to take any step towards the possibility of being caught in "a snare of the devil" [1 Timothy 3:7].

We ought not to be fearful, or even nervous, about standing up to the devil. And there are no words that you need to say to the devil. Contrary to what the devil's publicity agents suggest, there is only one God. Only God is omnipotent and omniscient and omnipresent—and eternal. The devil is not any of those things: he is not all-powerful, not all-knowing, not present everywhere—and he is running out of time. So, as the apostle Peter wrote, the devil "prowls around like a roaring lion, seeking someone to devour." But there is so much for the devil to do! So many calls to make, so many appointments to keep, and he has only so much power, and so much knowledge. And he is not able to be everywhere at the same time. And he is running out of time.

And so we are instructed to simply "resist him, firm in your faith" [1 Peter 5:8,9]. It won't take long for him to see that he would be wasting his precious time on you. "The full armour of God" is a great set of armour. It is all that we need to be brave and bold [Ephesians 6:12-18]. So don't run away. Just stand there!

PERSONAL NOTE: One of the ways you can tell that it is a devilish attack you are currently experiencing is to treat it exactly *as* such. If you are correct, and the devil or his cohorts are indeed at work on you, and on the chessboard of your mind (see the 7th Bit), the hellish experience will tend to end very abruptly. I think the point is that when we deliberately resist the devil's suggestions, we demonstrate to him and his gang that any further efforts will be a waste of their time. In my experience, once that roaring lion discerns that you really do mean to resist him, he moves on to more hopeful hunting grounds, thus bringing your devilish encounter to an abrupt end.

The 27th Bit: **TIME TO RUN**

In regard to all "youthful passions" and worldly temptations, Joseph in Egypt serves as an excellent example of how to respond.

> Genesis 39:11,12
> But one day, when [Joseph] went into the house to do his work and none of the men of the house was there in the house, [his boss's wife] caught him by his garment, saying, "Lie with me." But he left his garment in her hand and <u>fled</u> and <u>got out</u> of the house.

In both of the apostle Paul's letters to Timothy, he set out practical instructions for the actions that Joseph exemplified.

> 1 Timothy 6:11
> But as for you, O man of God, flee these things.[8]
> Pursue righteousness, godliness, faith[9], love, steadfastness, gentleness.

> 2 Timothy 2:22
> So flee youthful passions and pursue righteousness, faith, love, and peace, along with those who call on the Lord from a pure heart.

When our own lusts and passions are coming on to us, the thing we must do is to not just stand there, but Joseph-like, to get out of there!

The 28th Bit: BECOMING SOMETHING

We should perhaps always have a goal. Whether your specific current goal is a well-developed, daily "time with God," or the completion of a half-marathon, or reading *"War and Peace,"* or sailing around the world, here is a three-part recipe for successfully accomplishing a goal.

1. Get a plan

   A plan for accomplishing your goal is essential. Essential too, in the case of a very big goal, is a string of sub-plans. To illustrate, in 1978 I became interested in running a marathon. I was reading a 1977 bestseller entitled, *The Complete Book of Running*, by James

---

[8] You have to read this verse in its context to see exactly what "these things" are. Actually, it's a bit complicated.

[9] Or, "faithfulness," as explained in the 34th Bit. The same word occurs in the next verse cited: 2 Timothy 2:22.

F. Fixx. In this dazzling new book, the author wrote that to be able to complete a marathon (26.2 miles; 42.195 kilometers), you needed to develop the strength and endurance to run "10 miles and still feel springy." (The dust jacket of Fixx's book mentioned that the author ran 10 miles every day, and featured a black and white photo of Fixx running toward the camera and looking very definitely springy.) So I made "10 miles and still springy" a sub-goal, and I got right to it.

My "10 miles and springy" sub-plan didn't go well. In time, I came to see that the bad outcome was caused by a deadly combination of enthusiasm and ignorance. I quickly got up to running eight miles a day, and I was feeling great about it. So enthusiastically I went out for my eighth eight-mile run in 10 days. Picking up the pace on my way up a hill, my right shin suddenly hurt like crazy, as if someone whacked me from behind with a hockey stick. It was a stress fracture; not good news for a budding marathoner. I was completely sidelined from all running for three months. (Rats!) On the bright side, the 90-day interruption gave me lots of time to do more reading on how to train for a marathon, and how not to.

2. Love the vision

To stick to your plan, you need to develop a clear vision of success—and you need to nurture your love for that success. Read motivating books, and re-read them. Subscribe to magazines that support the vision, and absorb them. Attend workshops. Join a group. Watch videos. You need to put time and effort into preserving this new great love of your heart.

3. Hate the Opposite

Your love of your vision is what will *pull* you on to success. At the same time, a well-developed, carefully-nurtured hatred of failing can *push* you along the same road. Most of us have a natural

63

talent for hating things. All sorts of things. Spiders and snakes are both popular choices. These days the word "hate" shows up in all sorts of negative ways. But, in some circumstances, hatred is just the thing. In the Book of Proverbs, we are told that "the fear of the Lord is hatred of evil." Hating pride, hating arrogance and hating perverted speech are good things [Proverbs 8:13]. So add the prospect of failing to accomplish your goal to the list of things you hate.

The 29th Bit: BODY BRIBING

Actually, there are *four* points to the 28th Bit recipe for successfully accomplishing a goal. But the fourth point is controversial, because bribery is involved, so it gets a Bit of its own.

Biblically, bribery is a wicked thing. But when Scripture speaks of bribery, it is referring to the bribing of humans.

> Proverbs 15:27
> Whoever is greedy for unjust gain troubles his own household, but he who hates bribes will live.

If hating bribes is life-giving, then loving bribes is "the way of death" [Proverbs 14:12].

> Ecclesiastes 7:7
> Surely oppression drives the wise into madness, and a bribe corrupts the heart.

Since bribes corrupt a human heart, then a human with a new heart (see the 6th Bit) should be very, very leery of bribery.

On the other hand, bribing your dog is *not* a wicked thing, if, for example, your dog needs to get into your car for a drive to the veterinarian's clinic. In my opinion, bribing your body is also not wicked (see the 8th Bit). So I suggest you go ahead! Offer a bribe to that stubborn and lazy donkey that is your "flesh." You need your body's cooperation in order to get out the door for a run, or to the gym, or to the pool. If you promise your body a great dessert at the evening meal, it will quite likely oblige you. Other bribes that might appeal to your body are an extra long shower, or sleeping in the next morning, or booking a professional massage.

In my experience, human bodies are shamelessly susceptible to bribes, as are donkeys, and other stubborn animals. For the sake of your cause, take advantage of this glaring character weakness.

The 30th Bit: **PEACEMAKING**

The author of the New Testament letter "James," who identifies himself as "a servant of God and the Lord Jesus Christ" [James 1:1], (and who is thought to be the natural half-brother of Jesus), provided a very helpful description of what he called "the wisdom from above."

> James 3:16–18
> … where jealousy and selfish ambition exist, there will be disorder and every vile practice. But the wisdom from above is first pure, then peaceable, gentle, open to reason, full of mercy and good fruits, impartial and sincere. And a harvest of righteousness is sown in peace by those who make peace.

Early in my pastoral experience, I learned to lean heavily on this description of that sort of wisdom. In fact, I memorized that section of James 3, and then regularly used it to guide me in prayer, especially as I was driving to meet a challenging someone, or as I waited in my office for the same sort of person to arrive for an appointment.

Over and over again, this description directed me through many tense moments of difficult and potentially explosive pastoral conversations. Often (although not always!), the happy result was what James called, "a harvest of righteousness," which is so much better than the experience of an angry person storming out the door. As Jesus said "Blessed are the peacemakers" [Matthew 5:9].

The 31st Bit: DECIDING PRINCIPLES

How does a Christian ensure that, in regard to a decision that needs to be made, he or she is making that decision in accord with the will of God? I recommend three principles.

1. *The principle of submission*

    Submit the whole matter, and your whole self, to God. Often this is the only principle you need. If what you are wondering about doing (or not doing) is plainly a choice between obeying or disobeying God's commandments, the right choice is obvious. We must obey God, who blesses obedience and curses disobedience [Jeremiah 17:5-8]. So choose to do the right thing! Choose life [Deuteronomy 30:19,20]. Choose the blessing of God.

    An important part of our obedience must be to honour and in some cases obey those in authority over us. For example, a child is instructed to obey his or her parents [Ephesians 6:1-4]. A person who is no longer a child is still commanded to honour his or her father and mother [Exodus 20:12]. And, of course, there are other instructions of the same sort addressed to other segments of society: for example, wives, church members, citizens [Ephesians 5:22-24; Hebrews 13:17; Romans 13:1,2].

2. *The principle of counsel*

This second principle is sometimes necessary because the decision you are facing is not a moral issue—not a question of *right or wrong*. It's a question of *this or that*; a question of choosing this good thing to do, or that good thing to do, or neither thing, or both things. This question requires discernment, for the question is not to act righteously or otherwise, but to act wisely or otherwise. For such decision-making, the Book of Proverbs suggests seeking out godly advice.

> Proverbs 11:14
> Where there is no guidance, a people falls, but in <u>an abundance of counsellors</u> there is safety.

> Proverbs 15:22
> Without counsel plans fail, but with <u>many advisers</u> they succeed.

> Proverbs 20:18
> Plans are established <u>by counsel; by wise guidance</u> wage war.

When it is time for us to make a decision, we should seek out two or three or four people we consider wise, and ask each one of them for advice. (Perhaps coffee should be involved.)

Generally speaking, an odd number of wise counsellors (three or five, perhaps) is better than an even number, just as a consensus is better than a tie. But what if it *is* a tie? Or what if your counsellors all agree that this is a decision you simply need to make for yourself, since both of the options are, in themselves, wise choices. What then?

3. *"The third principle"*

This third principle is illustrated in the life of David, the King of Israel.

> 2 Samuel 7:1-3
> Now when the king lived in his house and the LORD had given him rest from all his surrounding enemies, the king said to Nathan the prophet, "See now, I dwell in a house of cedar, but the ark of God dwells in a tent." And Nathan said to the king, <u>"Go, do all that is in your heart</u>, for the LORD is with you".

Note that it was Nathan the prophet—David's spiritual authority, and his personal source of spiritual wisdom—that David consulted. I think it is then safe to assume that David had already implemented the first two principles by this point in the story. So now he had arrived at the third.

Whatever were the details of Nathan's roles in David's life until this time, it is generally our adherence to the first two principles that qualifies us to resort to the third principle. In other words, the third principle is to be followed only as the third principle in the important process of discerning the will of God. So I state it this way.

> THE THIRD PRINCIPLE
> In discerning the will of God in regard to a specific choice that must be made, a person who has wholeheartedly submitted himself to the authority of the Word of God, and to the authorities placed over him by God, <u>and</u> who has sought and received godly counsel regarding the choice from some number of wise people, should, as an act of faith in God, "do all that is in [his] heart."

And once we have followed our hearts according to the third principle? We must trust in the providence of God. The verses that immediately follow David's interaction with Nathan provide us with an example of God's specific intervention in the circumstance of David following the desire of his heart into an action that was contrary to God's will [2 Samuel 7:4-17].

The 32ⁿᵈ Bit: "MATEO": GIFTS GOD GIVES

I preached a three-week, four-part Sunday morning sermon series in the spring of 2010 (April 18, 25; May 2; www.wlachurch.org) about "sowing the seeds" that God has provided for a "harvest" he intends us to "reap." The sermons were based on these five verses:

> 2 Corinthians 9:6-10
> The point is this: whoever <u>sows sparingly</u> will also <u>reap sparingly</u>, and whoever <u>sows bountifully</u> will also <u>reap bountifully</u>. Each one must give as he has decided in his heart, not reluctantly or under compulsion, for God loves a cheerful giver. And God is able to make all grace abound to you, so that having all sufficiency in all things at all times, you may abound in every good work. As it is written, "He has distributed freely, he has given to the poor; his righteousness endures forever." He who supplies <u>seed to the sower</u> and bread for food will supply and multiply your <u>seed for sowing</u> and increase <u>the harvest of your righteousness.</u>

In the years that followed, these West London sermons have been mostly remembered for my use of the acronym MATEO, which I devised[10] to denote the gifts that God gives each one of us specifically as "seed for sowing." In other words, the gifts given to us by God can be used for more than the meeting of our own needs (*"having all sufficiency"* ..."*bread for food*"). The variety of gifts God gives us can, and should, be used for "sowing seed" and "reaping bountifully". (It was a happy little detail that the word "MATEO" is the European version, in Serbian and Spanish, for example, of the Hebrew name meaning "gift of Yahweh." The English equivalent is the name "Matthew.")

The specific gifts of God that were profiled in this sermon series were <u>M</u>oney, <u>A</u>bilities, <u>T</u>ime, <u>E</u>nergy and <u>O</u>pportunities. Each of these God-given gifts can be used for meeting our own personal and family needs ("bread for food"), or as "seed to sow" in the hope of additional "harvests of righteousness." Those sermons were easily my favourite "stewardship" series, for they explained that the biblical principles of stewardship stretch well past the realm of finances to the use of all God-given seeds for sowing and reaping.

Practically speaking, what that means is that every MATEO-type gift we receive from God is given to us both for the meeting of our own needs (and our family's needs), and for the privilege of getting in on a harvest. It is God's intention that we perform certain good works. The apostle Paul explains that these good works are prepared for us in advance!

---

10 I must say that, in my opinion, my "devising" of the acronym MATEO was a gift God gave me to give to the church. The experience of writing and then preaching those sermons remains a personal highlight of my years of leading West London. To God be the glory. Following the MATEO experience, God did do great things for WLA, just like in Psalm 126, the "shouts of joy" psalm.

> Ephesians 2:10
> For we are his workmanship, created in Christ Jesus for <u>good works, which God prepared beforehand</u>, that we should walk in them.

The good works we are "created in Christ Jesus" to accomplish are prepared in advance, and are provided to us by God in the form of money, abilities, time, energy and opportunities.

The 33rd Bit: HANDLEBARS

One of the things that you really should remember in learning to ride a bicycle is to keep both of your hands firmly on the handlebars. Something similar is involved in becoming a biblically-sound believer in Christ. But there is more than one set of handlebars to grip.

On beyond bicycle riding, there are handlebars made of two plainly-stated Bible truths which are both obviously essential to the faith, but which seem to contradict each other. For example, the "one-ness" and the "three-ness" of God [Deuteronomy 6:4; Matthew 28:18].

Another instance of handlebars is the personhood of Jesus Christ, who is genuinely divine and genuinely human, "truly God" and "truly a man" [John 10:29,30; Philippians 2:6,7].

Yet another pair is the individuality and the corporate identity of each Christian. His or her own physical body is a temple of the Holy Spirit [1 Corinthians 6:19], but he himself, or she herself, is a "member" (a body part) of a church: which is called "the body of Christ" and "God's temple" [1 Corinthians 3:16; 12:12,14].

In every case, both handgrips must be firmly and whole-heartedly held on to. Metaphorically speaking, to hold tightly to one handlebar, but only lightly to the other, can make for a wobbly ride, and maybe a quick trip to the Emergency Room.

As we sort out what we believe, we should recognize a set of handlebars whenever we come across one.

A COMMON EXAMPLE: In my opinion, serious theological confusion comes from pairing up "the absolute sovereignty of God" with the "free will" of human beings (see Piece #17 on the freedom of the will). But to cut to the chase, here I state my opinion that if "the absolute sovereignty of God" is one handgrip, the other corresponding handgrip is not the complicated thing called "free will," but rather "the moral responsibility" of each of us.

CHAPTER FIVE:
ELEVEN CONTROVERSIAL BITS

The 34th Bit: THE SON OF GOD'S FAITH

As a word of caution, this Bit is a bit more complicated than your average Bit. But, as it goes sometimes, sorting out a complication can bring a very rich reward. This one establishes and strengthens and explains our conviction that the faithfulness of the Lord Jesus is the foundation, or the exact centre, of our life of faith in Christ, and that we are much more indebted to him than many of us might realize.

One of the first Bible verses I memorized as a new Christian was Galatians 2:20. In those days, I was a "King James Version guy."

> I am crucified with Christ: nevertheless I live; yet not I, but Christ liveth in me: and the life which I now live in the flesh <u>I live by the faith of the Son of God,</u> who loved me, and gave himself for me.

This verse immediately became one of my favourite Bible verses, for obvious reasons. But there was a lot about this verse that I wasn't sure I understood. For example, what it meant to "live by the faith of the Son of God." "The faith *of* the Son of God?" I wondered. "I thought I was to live by *my* faith!"

A few years later, I switched to the New American Standard Bible, the "NASB," or as some of my new friends called it, "the nas-bee." In that modern translation, the second half of Galatians 2:20 was worded slightly differently: "… the life which I now live in the flesh *I live by faith in the Son of God*, who loved me and gave Himself up for me." That seemed to make more sense.

But then I learned a tiny bit of Greek. I learned that the Greek word "π ι σ τ ι σ" (*pistis,*) which is translated as "faith," can also be—and sometimes *should* be—translated "faithfulness." For example, the NASB (and other modern versions) translates Romans 3:3 like this: "What then? If some did not believe, their unbelief will not nullify the faithfulness ("*pistis*") of God, will it?"

Meanwhile, back in the early 1600s, the King James Version of the same Bible verse read like this: "For what if some did not believe? Shall their unbelief make the faith ("*pistis*") of God without effect?" And there are other scriptural statements that receive the same treatments in the KJV, and in modern versions:

> Galatians 5:22,23
> "the fruit of the Spirit is love, joy, peace, longsuffering, gentleness, goodness, faith (*pistis*), meekness, temperance …" [KJV]

> Galatians 5:22,23
> "the fruit of the Spirit is love, joy, peace, patience, kindness, goodness, faithfulness (*pistis*), gentleness, self control … " [NASB]

If someone asks what difference it makes to translate the Greek word as "faith" instead of "faithfulness," I answer that the difference is what it leads us to think about how we are actually able to live for Christ. In Galatians 2:20, to *"live by faith in the Son of God"* seems to be saying that the ongoing strength of our relationship with Christ depends upon *our* faith in him. In other words, if our faith in Christ is strong, we will live for Christ well; if our faith in Christ is only so-so, we will live for Christ less well. Of course, both of those maxims are true. But those truths might not be ones that the apostle Paul explained in Galatians 2:20.

On the other hand, to *"live by the faithfulness of the Son of God"* would mean that to live for Christ at all, our lives, and even our faith(!), must be empowered by Christ's faithfulness. This is also true, and I think it *is* what the apostle Paul specifically was saying in Galatians 2:20.

There are other New Testament instances of the same sort of translation choice.

> Ephesians 3:11,12
> According to the eternal purpose which he [God] purposed in Christ Jesus our Lord: in whom we have boldness and access with confidence by the faith of him. [KJV]

> Ephesians 3:11,12
> This was according to the eternal purpose that he [God] has realized in Christ Jesus our Lord, in whom we have boldness and access with confidence through our faith in him ... [NASB]

The translators make their choice, but if we choose to understand the verses in the alternate way, Paul's statement runs like this:

Ephesians 3:11,12
… Christ Jesus our Lord, in whom we have boldness and access with confidence <u>by his faithfulness</u>.

To me, this is very thrilling stuff. I picture two believers entering the throne room of God, with two different understandings of Ephesians 3:12, or Galatians 2:20. Both believers are feeling confident about approaching God. Both of them are carrying a large placard, to explain their confidence.

The "faith" man's placard reads:

> I HAVE ACCESS BECAUSE I HAVE FAITH

The "faithfulness" man's placard reads:

> I HAVE ACCESS BECAUSE CHRIST IS FAITHFUL

These two bold, confident men are not thinking the same way about their right to enter God's presence! One is putting his confidence in his own faith. The other is putting his confidence in Christ's faithfulness.

EXTRA ASSIGNMENT: Consider Romans 3:21,22 and Philippians 3:8,9.

FINAL NOTE: Not every New Testament mention of "faith in Christ" can be legitimately given this treatment. But the way to know where it *is* valid to re-translate the word "faith" to "faithfulness" can be discovered very simply by consulting a King James Version of the Bible. (Maybe you can borrow your grandfather's.) The modern translations, in some places, tinker with the prepositions, switching the "of" to "in" (that is, switching from the Greek genitive case to the Greek dative case), although there is no manuscript warrant to do so. But the good old KJV always translates the "of" (that is, the genitive case) as "of." Always.

The 35th Bit: WHAT GIFTS PROVE

In Galatians 5, the apostle Paul refers to "the fruit of the Spirit," and itemizes it as "love, joy, peace, patience, goodness, faithfulness, gentleness and self-control." In Ephesians 5, he refers to "the fruit of the light," describing it as "all that is good and right and true." It is easy enough to see that all these details of the fruit God produces are aspects of Christ's own character. Who was more loving than Jesus? More patient than Jesus? More faithful? More gentle? More self-controlled? More good and right and true?

As the fruit of Christlikeness is produced in us, we resemble Jesus more and more. Without that fruit, people can't tell by looking that we are, in fact, believers in Christ [John 13:34,35]. So Jesus said to his first followers, "By this my Father is glorified, that you bear much fruit and so prove to be my disciples" [John 15:8].

If the fruit of the Spirit authenticates our faith in Christ, what about the gifts of the Spirit? [Romans 12:4-8; 1 Corinthians 12:4-11; Ephesians 4:11-13; 1 Peter 4:10,11] The Bible reveals that spiritual gifts have a very different personal significance than "spiritual fruit." King Saul was a prophet [1 Samuel 19:21-24], and prophecy is a gift of the Spirit. Judas Iscariot was an apostle [Mark 3:13-19], and apostleship is a spiritual gift. But both men, spiritually gifted as they were, were utterly rejected by God. The gifts of the Spirit do not authenticate the legitimacy of our claim to belong to Christ. The fruit of the Spirit does.

What then do gifts of the Spirit authenticate? Just this: that in that particular place and at that particular time, through some particular person(s), the Holy Spirit was at work, giving gifts by which the kingdom of God is strengthened, the testimony of the Lord is proclaimed, and God is glorified through Jesus Christ.

> 1 Corinthians 12:4–11
> Now there are varieties of gifts, but the same Spirit; and there are varieties of service, but the same Lord; and there are varieties of activities, but it is the same God who empowers them all in everyone. To each is given the manifestation of the Spirit for the common good. For to one is given through the Spirit the utterance of wisdom, and to another the utterance of knowledge according to the same Spirit, to another faith by the same Spirit, to another gifts of healing by the one Spirit, to another the working of miracles, to another prophecy, to another the ability to distinguish between spirits, to another various kinds of tongues, to another the interpretation of tongues. All these are empowered by one and the same Spirit, who apportions to each one individually as he wills.

The 36th Bit: **IF I SHOULD DIE**

The words sound strange to me now, but when I was very young, my mother taught me to pray this bedtime prayer:

> Now I lay me down to sleep. I pray the Lord my soul to keep.
>
> If I should die before I wake, I pray the Lord my soul to take.

My mother had learned this prayer when she was a child. It was a bedtime prayer from the olden days, when cholera, mumps, tuberculosis, and other diseases could wipe out large swaths of a town's young children. So the children were taught to pray about dying.

CONTROVERSIAL BITS

What actually happens when you die? How does the Lord "take" your soul? There are New Testament statements on the subject, and more than a few opinions on what those statements mean. But two things are clear.

Firstly, people who have actually been regenerated (see the 6th Bit) "fall asleep in Christ." So we are told both by Luke, the author of Acts, and by Paul, the apostle.

> Acts 7:60
> And falling to his knees [Stephen] cried out with a loud voice, "Lord, do not hold this sin against them." And when he had said this, he fell asleep.
>
> Acts 13:36
> For David, after he had served the purpose of God in his own generation, fell asleep and was laid with his fathers and saw corruption.
>
> 1 Corinthians 15:6
> Then [Christ] appeared to more than five hundred brothers at one time, most of whom are still alive, though some have fallen asleep.
>
> 1 Thessalonians 4:13-15
> But we do not want you to be uninformed, brothers, about those who are asleep, that you may not grieve as others do who have no hope. For since we believe that Jesus died and rose again, even so, through Jesus, God will bring with him those who have fallen asleep. For this we declare to you by a word from the Lord, that we who are alive, who are left until the coming of the Lord, will not precede those who have fallen asleep.

We should note that Luke and Paul do not write that the *bodies* of the saints "fall asleep." Both writers state that it is the dead person himself who "sleeps."

Secondly, believers who die, having "fallen asleep in Christ," that is, having actually died, rise to life on the day of "the coming of the Lord" [1 Thessalonians 4:15,16].

Jesus himself declared:

> John 5:28,29
> ... an hour is coming when all who are in the tombs will hear his voice and come out, those who have done good to the resurrection of life, and those who have done evil to the resurrection of judgment.

> John 6: 39,40,44
> And this is the will of him who sent me, that I should lose nothing of all that he has given me, but <u>raise it up at the last day.</u> For my Father's will is that everyone who looks to the Son and believes in him shall have eternal life, and <u>I will raise them up on the last day.</u> ... No one can come to me unless the Father who sent me draws him. And <u>I will raise him up on the last day.</u>

On the day of humanity's first appearance in the world, the Lord formed man (the actual Hebrew word is "adam) "of dust from the ground" and "breathed into his nostrils the breath [or spirit] of life, and the man became a living creature," or, as other modern English translations word it, "a living soul" [Genesis 2:7]. At the moment of a human being's death, the body "of dust" and "the breath [or spirit] of life" become separated. But on "the day of resurrection," Christ will appear "in a moment, in the twinkling of an eye," like a playwright walking out on the stage when the play is over, and all "predeceased" humans will be raised to life.

> John 5:28,29
> ... all who are in the tombs will hear his voice and come out, those who have done good to the resurrection of life, and those who have done evil to the resurrection of judgment.

Now *that* will be a day, and a moment: the day and the hour of the return of Jesus—and the moment of the resurrection of all human souls.

Back in my days of student ministries, when I explained this whole concept to high school and university students, I called it "The Lesser Zap Theory." I don't think Arthur C. Custance ever even considered calling it that. But it was he from whom I learned the concept, in his book *Journey Out of Time*.[11] His idea was that we cannot be "living souls," that is, actual human beings, without both a physical body and a God-given spirit; a "breath of life." So when the two are separated by death, the body goes into the grave, or the crematorium, or whatever, and the spirit goes forward in time to the day of resurrection, which is the day of the Lord's return [1 Thessalonians 4:13-17]. The New Testament people said that those who have died are "asleep." Science fiction fans might say that they have traveled forward in time to "the resurrection day." In my vocabulary, people who experience this "journey out of time" are said to be "zapped."

The 37th Bit: SABBATH-KEEPING

It was a very big, bad deal to Robert Murray M'Cheyne, in the 1830's and 40's, that the government of Scotland began to permit trains to

---

11 All of Custance's books and his "Doorway Papers" are still in print, and available in several formats at custance.org.

run on Sundays. The Lord's Day! The Sabbath! From his position as the minister of the Presbyterian Church in Dundee, he protested with scathing denunciations, from the pulpit and in the newspapers.

But if "Sabbath-breaking" is as egregious a sin as M'Cheyne declared, what are we to make of the following two statements of the apostle Paul?

> Romans 14:5,6
> One person esteems one day as better than another, while another esteems all days alike. Each one should be <u>fully convinced in his own mind</u>. <u>The one who observes the day, observes it in honour of the Lord.</u> The one who eats, eats in honour of the Lord, since he gives thanks to God, while the one who abstains, abstains in honour of the Lord and gives thanks to God.

Here, Paul compares a solemn commitment to the keeping of a special day (for example, "the Sabbath") to a solemn commitment about foods we do or do not eat. Someone might say, "But the Sabbath is different. Remembering and observing the Sabbath is one of the Ten Commandments!" And, of course, it is [Exodus 20:8-11; Deuteronomy 5:12-15]. But the apostle Paul also wrote,

> Colossians 2:16
> Therefore let no one pass judgment on you in questions of food and drink, or with regard to a festival or a new moon <u>or a Sabbath</u>.

So then, what about that? Is a faithful follower of Christ commanded to keep the weekly Sabbath? Personally, I don't think so; not as a matter of keeping God's Law. The principle of a weekly day of rest remains with us, for it is a universal principle, and continues to be a good and healthy principle to live by [Genesis 2:1-3]. Like the Old Testament tithing laws, the Sabbath laws establish the picture of the details of the life of a godly man or woman living the life. Thus, the good stewardship of our time and money is taught. But the Old Testament Sabbath laws have been revoked, as were the Old Testament food laws [Mark 7:14-19].

In Hebrew 3:7-11, the writer quotes Psalm 95:5-11. Hebrews 3:11 quotes the Holy Spirit, who in Psalm 95 declares, "As I swore in my wrath, 'They shall not enter my rest.'" This Old Testament quotation is specifically discussed in Hebrews 3 and 4, which declare that "there remains a Sabbath rest for the people of God" (verse 9). Taken on their own, those ten words might be thought to contradict Romans 14, and especially Colossians 2:16. But the context of Hebrews 4 makes plain that the Old Testament references to this rest, this "Sabbath," are being used to explain the particular rest that God gave his people, beginning on the day that Joshua led them across the Jordan River and into the Promised Land—that is, a rest from centuries of Egyptian slavery, and decades of wilderness-wandering. But when the Lord Jesus came to inaugurate the New Covenant, he offered rest from the weight of the burden of obedience to the ceremonies of the Old Testament Law. Jesus said,

> Matthew 11:28-30
> Come to me, all who labor and are heavy laden, and
> <u>I will give you rest</u>. Take my yoke upon you, and
> learn from me, for I am gentle and lowly in heart,
> and <u>you will find rest for your souls</u>. For my yoke is
> easy, and my burden is light.

This is the "Sabbath rest" offered to all who believe in Christ, that is, to all who believe and entrust themselves to "the guarantor of a better covenant" [Hebrews 7:22]; all those who take the yoke of Jesus upon themselves in order to be his slaves (= "his slaves") rather than slaves of sin; serving him rather than any other master. This is "the Sabbath" that Jesus offers; the "Sabbath rest" that those who belong to Christ are invited to live in. The "Promised Land" that was given to Israel is a picture of life as a Christian. Christ invites us to enter this better rest, for his is a better covenant, and he is "gentle and lowly in heart." And his rest is a rest for our souls.

The 38th Bit: FOREKNOWING THOSE

Very often, when a discussion of the sovereignty of God and the predestination of the elect becomes a debate, someone brings up the topic of foreknowledge. This generally leads the discussion to Romans 8:29. There are three other "foreknowledge" New Testament verses to consider, but this is the verse that also mentions predestination, and so gets most of the attention.

> Romans 8:29
> For <u>those whom he foreknew</u> he also predestined to be conformed to the image of his Son, in order that he might be the firstborn among many brothers.

Very often, the debater's intended use of this verse is to prove that God's predestination of his chosen people is not what some people think. "The only people God specifically predestines to be saved," the debater argues, "are those people that he already knows will believe in him." Often he or she goes on. "God in his infinite wisdom knows everything that is going to happen long before it does. In actual fact, God chooses everyone. Everyone in the world is chosen by God. But God leaves it to every individual to decide, by his or her own free will, whether or not to choose God. The all-knowing God foreknows that some people never will put their free will to work in that way."

The problem with this line of thinking is that it is not at all what Romans 8:29 says. Here are two things that this verse *does* say:

- <u>God "foreknows" people; not actions</u>.

   He "pre-knows" people, not what people will someday do. Of course, he also does know beforehand everything that people will do. But that's not what Paul the apostle is talking about in Romans 8.

- <u>God predestines some people; not all people</u>.

   Some people; that is, the people "whom he foreknows." Verse 29 does not say that God predestines people whom he knows will believe in him. Of course, God does know that those people will believe in him, primarily because he knows whom he has predestined. From "before the foundation of the world," he has chosen them to be "holy and blameless before him" [Ephesians 1:4].

The 39th Bit: ALL THINGS FOR GOOD

> Romans 8:28
> And we know that for those who love God all things work together for good, for those who are called according to his purpose.

The Bible verse often featured on many a greeting card, and many a coffee mug, seems, to many people, to be an assurance that God is in the business of making his people healthy and prosperous for all the happy days of their fun-filled lives. But the poverty and diseases and persecution of God's people around the world—in history and in today's news—challenge such an explanation of that particular Bible verse.

Purposely ignoring a statement in God's Word is as hazardous as misunderstanding it. So what about Romans 8:28? One of the most significant details of the verse is that it precedes Roman 8:29, which identifies the specific "good" that God is said, in verse 28, to make all things work together for, namely the good of "being conformed to the image of [God's] Son."

So we see that God's sovereign purpose in ordering the details of our lives is to make us, in heart and mind and action, increasingly more like Jesus.

> Hebrews 12:5–11
> And have you forgotten the exhortation that addresses you as sons?
>
> "My son, do not regard lightly the discipline of the Lord, nor be weary when reproved by him. For <u>the Lord disciplines the one he loves,</u> and chastises every son whom he receives." It is for discipline that you have to endure. God is treating you as sons. For what son is there whom his father does not discipline? If you are left without discipline, in which all have participated, then you are illegitimate children and not sons. Besides this, we have had earthly fathers who disciplined us and we respected them. Shall we not much more be subject to the Father of spirits and live? For they disciplined us for a short time as it seemed best to them, but <u>he disciplines us for our good, that we may share his holiness.</u> For the moment all discipline seems painful rather than pleasant, but later it yields the peaceful fruit of righteousness to those who have been trained by it.

The 40th Bit: EXPLAINING MISERY

Jonathan Edwards, the long-time pastor of the Congregational church in Northampton, Massachusetts (1727-1748), wrote the following words concerning an effective presentation of the gospel, which is "the power of God for salvation" [Romans 1:16]:

> To suppose <u>mercy without supposing misery</u>, or <u>pity without calamity</u>, is a contradiction; therefore men cannot look upon themselves as proper objects of mercy unless they first <u>know themselves to be miserable</u>; and so, unless this be the case, it is <u>impossible that they should come to God for mercy</u> …
>
> They must be sensible that the guilt of sin makes them <u>miserable creatures</u>, whatever temporal enjoyments they have; that they can be no other than <u>miserable, undone creatures</u>, so long as God is angry with them; that they are without strength, and must perish, and that eternally, unless God help them.

These thoughts are a long way away from the depictions and descriptions of the gospel—and the God of the gospel—with which we 21st century North American Christians busy ourselves. No wonder. The great big challenge of turning a casual conversation with friends to the topic of "spiritual things" is difficult enough without including the idea that people must come to see that they are "miserable, undone creatures"—and that "God is angry with them." It is not nice talk. But it was not Jonathan Edwards who first said, "Whoever believes in the Son has eternal life; whoever does not obey the Son shall not see life, but <u>the wrath of God remains on him</u>" [John 3:36].

Jonathan Edwards took that sort of Bible verse seriously; so seriously that he faithfully incorporated such biblical statements into his theology, his writing, his biblical counsel, and his preaching. Of course, it is a good idea to stay clear on the fact that Edwards was doing his gospel work 300 years ago. But it is also a good idea to choose carefully the words we use to describe the *biblical* details of the true condition of actual unregenerate human beings (see the 5th Bit). In other words, we are wise to choose carefully the words and phrases we use to explain the complicated matter of how very bad "the bad news" is. For we must explain, when we see the opportunity, because people must understand the extent of "the bad news" in order to appreciate "the good news" that is the gospel.

Mr. Edwards used the words "misery" and "calamity" to explain the realities of the human plight, and the words "mercy" and "pity" to explain the remedies that actual humans can experience through the kindness of God. Does that mean that we should use these same words? Surely the Bible makes clear that Mr. Edwards is right about the true nature of God, and the true condition of humans, and the true grace of God. And we modern Christians must explain, whenever we have the opportunity, the great truth of the gospel; thoughtfully, graciously and lovingly. But we are not talking to people living in the New England colonies in the 1730's, 40's and 50's.

When in Rome, even if we determine to live not as the Romans do,[12] we really should learn to speak to our new neighbours in Italian.

The 41st Bit: THE PROMISED LIFE

Sometimes what we read in the Bible does not mean what we think it means. A general notion about some portion of the Bible can become entrenched in the minds of a large number of Christians without actually being a correct notion. An example of this is the widely-held notion that "crossing the Jordan River and entering the Promised Land" is a metaphor for a Christian "crossing the river of death" to enter heaven.

The life in Canaan to which Joshua was leading the nation of Israel was actually nothing like what we believe about life in the heavenly realities. Living in Canaan turned out not to be a life with no death, no mourning,

---

[12] The expression *"When in Rome, do as the Romans do"* originated with something Augustine, the great North African church father, once wrote in a letter to a colleague, on the topic of the difference between the day of the week the Roman Christians fast, in contrast to the fast days of other Christians.

no praying, no pain; not a life in which "the former things [had] passed away" [Revelation 21:4]. Living in "the Promised Land" was much more like the life of this world's "sojourners and exiles," that is, the people of Christ [1 Peter 2:11]. Life in "the Holy Land" was filled with dangers to face, challenges to overcome, battles to fight and win or lose—and all kinds of ungodliness. Sometimes, large, long-term inconveniences were added to Israel's life as a result of their own failure to follow thoroughly God's explicit instructions [e.g. Deuteronomy 7:1,2,16; Joshua 9:1-27]. Sometimes Israel's battles were lost as the chastening of the Lord for Israel's over-confidence, or disobedience [Joshua 7:1-26; Hebrews 12:5-11]. "For the Lord disciplines the one he loves, and chastises every son whom he receives" [Hebrews 12:6].

In his long career as a military commander, Joshua (and his soldiers) successfully conquered 31 of the independent kingdoms they found in this land that God had given to Abraham and his descendants [Genesis 15:18-21]. But all those victories of Joshua did not mean the work was finished.

> Joshua 13:1,2
> Now Joshua was old and advanced in years, and the LORD said to him, "You are old and advanced in years, and <u>there remains yet very much land</u> to possess. This is the land that yet remains: all the regions of the Philistines, and all those of the Geshurites …

Every failure of Israel's army—every kingdom Israel left unconquered—became one more set of wicked, idolatrous influences. This problem remained for all of Joshua's life [Joshua 24:14-24].

As for us, the apostle Peter warns that "the passions of the flesh" that we do not learn to control will continue to "wage war against" us [1 Peter 2:11]. That is the reality of living the life that Christ gives us [John 10:10]. And the New Testament explains that these lives we live end, not with a boat ride across a river, but with a sleep, followed by a resurrection. (See the 36th Bit)

The 42nd Bit: THE GREAT ZAP THEORY

This particular Bit is about an audacious tool I invented (when I was young, and full of spit and vinegar) to teach students the doctrine of "glorification," and the details of glorification's relationship to justification and sanctification [1 Corinthians 15:50-53; 1 John 3:2]. Just imagine the audacity of a young Bible teacher daring to draw a two-dimensional graph to chart an individual's progress in sanctification, or "Christlikeness," (to be measured along the y-axis) over "time" (measured on the x-axis). So the graph is audacious. But was my understanding of glorification correct?

Justification, in the words of the Westminster Shorter Catechism, is "an act of God's free grace, wherein he pardoneth all our sins, and accepteth us as righteous in his sight, only for the righteousness of Christ imputed to us, and received by faith alone."

Justification is mentioned four times in Romans 5, and in numerous other places in the apostle Paul's letters[13]. On the audacious graph, the miracle of a person's justification is positioned at the bottom left corner of the graph (0,0). To be anywhere on the graph at all, even (0,0), means, as the Westminster theologians explained, that you *are* justified, that is, pardoned of all your sins and accepted as righteous in God's sight, because the righteousness of Christ has been imputed to you, through your faith in Christ.

Glorification is a word not found in the Westminster documents, but we can define it in the terminology that the documents use to elaborate on

---

[13] The Book of James also makes reference to justification [2:14-26]. In my opinion, James uses the same term in a slightly different sense, which has always confused students of the Bible. It still does these 2,000 years later. James' use of the word "justified" [James 2:21,24,25] is found in the context of his discussion of our relationship with faith and our works. In his way of saying things, there can be no certainty of our justification if we do not "have works" [verse 14]. These statements of James are very similar to the Lord's words, for example, about the "rich ruler." "I tell you, this man went down to his house justified, rather than the other ..." [Luke 18:14]

justification. For example, "The glorious fact that 'all those who have been justified in life, are, in death, made perfect in holiness and do immediately pass into glory. They are raised up in glory, openly acknowledged and acquitted in the day of judgment, and made perfectly blessed in the full enjoying of God to all eternity.'"

In other words, glorification is the work of God by which he completes the miraculous transformation of character that he makes possible for his people "in Christ" through the miracle of justification.

Our graph places glorification at (x,y), which is positioned, of course, at the top right corner of the graph, indicating that the person whose spiritual progress is being charted has reached the end of his life. That position (x,y) also indicates that every person on the graph (having been justified by God) is, at the end of his life, transformed into Christlikeness.

> Romans 8:30
> … those whom [God] <u>justified</u> he also <u>glorified.</u>
>
> Philippians 1:6
> … he who began a good work in you will bring it to <u>completion</u> at the day of Jesus Christ.
>
> 1 John 3:2
> Beloved, we are God's children now, and what we will be has not yet appeared; but we know that <u>when he appears we shall be like him</u>, because we shall see him as he is.

The audacious graph raises the question of what we Christians, living out our time on earth as the justified people of Christ, are supposed to be doing. The apostle John answers the question plainly.

> 1 John 3:3
> And everyone who thus hopes in [Christ] purifies himself as [Christ] is pure.

Everyone! The graph below charts the life experience of three (hypothetical) people who have been justified, and who may or may not have understood their own upcoming glorification, and their obligations in regard to it.

Here, the Westminster theologians are once again helpful. They explained that *sanctification* is the process by which those "who are once effectually called and regenerated, having a new heart and a new spirit created in them, are further sanctified, really and personally, through the virtue of Christ's death and resurrection, by His Word and Spirit dwelling in them: the dominion of the whole body of sin is destroyed, and the several lusts thereof are more and more weakened and mortified; and are more and more quickened and strengthened in all saving graces, to the practice of true holiness without which no man will see the Lord." The apostle Paul wrote of sanctification in Romans 6:19-22.

On the graph below, we see that "A" lived a very steady and "successful" life, always growing into conformity to the image of Christ. And we should say, good for him!

Christian "B" had a different experience. Her early days as a Christian were thrilling days, and she grew in her faith a great deal, on many spiritual levels. Her line on the graph shows what tragically happened when she was about a third of the way along her timeline. The graph reveals the sad fact that, at one point in her life as a Christian, "B"'s faith weakened almost to the point of collapse, with many of her holy attainments in Christlikeness lost. But, by the grace of God, "B" came to her senses, and repented of her waywardness [2 Timothy 2:25,26]. Happily, for all the time remaining for her, she grew and grew in Christlikeness, as she had done in the early days of her faith in Christ.

Christian "C" has yet a different story. He began well. Shortly after he was justified, he established himself in a healthy church, and surrounded himself with godly influences. For a while, "C" diligently sought maturity in his faith. But then, sadly—and not very far into his new life—he came under other influences. It started with a beautiful young woman, her rich family, her very cool friends, and a large sailboat. Much of "C"'s early enthusiasm for Christ eroded. Although he continued to serve and believe in Christ, he developed some limits to prevent himself, as he came to say it, from "taking his religion too far." Christian "C"'s moderation was admired by his new friends, and appreciated by the beautiful young woman. Of course, when "C"'s time came, he died. And by the astonishing grace of God, having been justified through faith, along with Christians "A" & "B," "C" got *zapped,* all the way up to the top right-hand corner of the graph.

Here then is the audacious graph, that charts the life trajectories of "A," "B" and "C."

THE GREAT ZAP THEORY

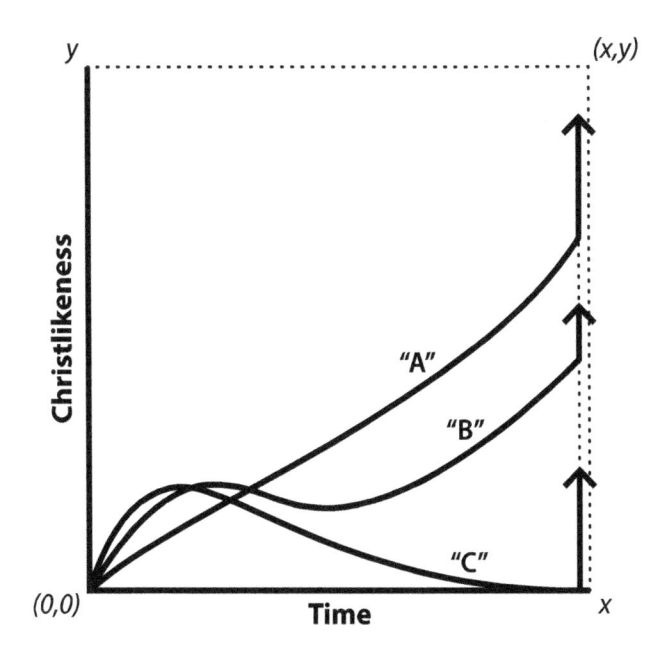

Obviously, the intended objective of all Christians should be to grow in sanctification to such an extent that, when their time on earth runs out, the glorification that immediately follows does not render that Christian almost totally unrecognizable. To put it another way, in terms of this graph, "the shorter your zap, the better you've lived for Christ."

Paul the apostle explained very plainly (to the churches in Rome and Corinth, for example) that there is no place for a casual attitude about our sanctification and spiritual growth.

> Romans 14:10–12
> … For we will all stand before the judgment seat of God; for it is written,
>
> "As I live, says the Lord, every knee shall bow to me, and every tongue shall confess to God." So then <u>each of us will give an account</u> of himself to God.
>
> 2 Corinthians 5:10
> … we must all appear before the judgment seat of Christ, so that <u>each one may receive what is due</u> for what he has done in the body, whether good or evil.

The 43rd Bit: ALL KINDS OF PEOPLE

> 2 Peter 3:9
> The Lord is not slow to fulfill his promise as some count slowness, but is patient toward you, <u>not wishing that any should perish, but that all should reach repentance.</u>
>
> 1 Timothy 2:3–6
> This is good, and it is pleasing in the sight of God

> our Savior, who <u>desires all people to be saved and to come to the knowledge of the truth</u>. For there is one God, and there is one mediator between God and men, the man Christ Jesus, who gave himself as <u>a ransom for all</u>, which is the testimony given at the proper time.

For the years of my life as a pastor, I found myself from time to time discussing these two passages. Often, the conversation was with somebody who had heard me assert that God has all things, in every way, under his control (as I did, for example, in Chapter 3 of *"Glory in the Face,"* especially pages 32-37.) On some occasions, that somebody approached me with sincere zeal—and sometimes with flushed face—and with a Bible open at 2 Peter 3:9. And he would declare, "God is not wishing that *any* should perish!"

My practice was to encourage that somebody to read the entire verse, and then to study the whole chapter, or better still, the entire epistle. At the very beginning of his letter, Peter stated that he was writing specifically to "those who have obtained a faith of equal standing with ours by the righteousness of our God and Saviour Jesus Christ,"—in other words, to authentic Christians, who had been given by God the same sort of faith as Peter and his fellow apostles[14] had "obtained." My point was that, at that time in the history of the work of the gospel, God communicated through the writing of the apostle Peter his intention that many more people would obtain this same "faith of equal standing" with the apostles of Christ, for "Yes," God was not wishing for any of them, any of *"his elect,"* to perish. (See Acts 11:18 and 18:10)

At other times, often with that same sincere zeal and flushed face, someone would approach me with a Bible open at 1 Timothy 2:3, and

---

14 Particularly, perhaps, James and John, as Peter refers to them in vss. 16-18. See also Matthew 17:1-8; Mark 9:1-8; Luke 9:27-36.

would read it to me with special emphasis on the words: "God our Savior desires *all* people to be saved". The ensuing dialogue between us would follow similar lines as the 2 Peter 3:9 conversation. But on 1 Timothy 2:3, I usually also explained one of the few things I know about New Testament Greek, particularly the Greek word translated into English as "all."

In Greek, the word is πασ (pronounced "pass"), and means "all," specifically either "all without exception," as in "all snowflakes are unique" or "all without distinction," as in "all professional hockey players have skates." In other words, according to the context, the Greek word πασ ("pass") can either be translated "all" or "all kinds of". So then, 1 Timothy 2:3 can be understood to mean, "God our Saviour desires *all kinds of people* to be saved." This corresponds to that spectacular vision described in the concluding book of the Bible.

> Revelation 7:9,10
> After this I looked, and behold, a great multitude that no one could number, from every nation, from all tribes and peoples and languages, standing before the throne and before the Lamb, clothed in white robes, with palm branches in their hands, and crying out with a loud voice, "Salvation belongs to our God who sits on the throne, and to the Lamb!"

A great multitude that no one could number! A multitude drawn from every nation, from all tribes and peoples and languages. A multitude appointed by God from every nation, to be saved by Jesus Christ through faith; appointed without distinction.

> Acts 13:48
> And when the Gentiles heard this, they began rejoicing and glorifying the word of the Lord, and <u>as many as were appointed to eternal life</u> believed.

CONTROVERSIAL BITS

The 44ᵗʰ Bit: **THAT FULL-GROWN MAN**

The apostle Paul, in his letter to the Ephesians, explained the assignments of "the apostles, the prophets, the evangelists, the shepherds and teachers" who had been personally given by Christ as gifts to the churches of Christ [Ephesians 4:11-13]. Paul was comparing these human "gifts" to the slaves that a conquering military leader might give to his friends, upon his return from war. These newly-enslaved people were considered an especially valuable part of the spoils of battle. Each of *these* new slaves, otherwise known as leaders in the church: apostles, prophets, evangelists, shepherds and teachers, were given the task of equipping "the saints for the work of ministry." Paul described the intended outcome of the slaves' assignment as "building up the body of Christ."

The next thing Paul wrote about in Ephesians 4 was Christ's purpose in giving these gifts. His purpose was, and is, that "we all attain to the unity of the faith and of the knowledge of the Son of God, to mature manhood, to the measure of the stature of the fullness of Christ, so that we may no longer be children, tossed to and fro by the waves and carried about by every wind of doctrine, by human cunning, by craftiness in deceitful schemes" [verses 13,14].

An interesting detail of the English translation of Paul's very long Greek sentence is that the phrase in verse 13 rendered as "mature manhood" is more plainly translated as "a full-grown man." (Perhaps it was in order to dodge current gender controversies that many modern translators have avoided altogether the words "man" and "manhood," and have chosen instead the words "mature adulthood," and "becoming mature". Nonetheless, the phrase the apostle actually used is most plainly translated "a full-grown man.")

However delicately—or offensively—translators do their translating, the general understanding of Paul's statement these days is, I think, that he is writing about the spiritual maturity of each individual member of the Ephesian church. But there is a problem with this general understanding. The spiritual maturity of individual Christians, whether male or female, *is* certainly being called for in this text:

> "… we all attain to the unity of the faith and of the knowledge of the Son of God… we may no longer be children… we are to grow up in every way into him" (vss.13-15)

But Paul's emphasis in Ephesians 4 is actually on a particular church: "one body… building up the body of Christ… the whole body, joined and held together… builds itself up in love" [Ephesians 4:4,12,16]. Any particular church of Jesus Christ, whether located in 1st century Ephesus or Rome or Jerusalem, or 21st century Shanghai or New Delhi or London.

So then it seems appropriate to understand the phrase "to mature manhood" (literally, "to a full-grown man") to be a reference to the *corporate* growth and development of an individual church, rather than the personal growth and development of an individual Christian. That church itself, whose "head" is Christ, must become "mature," or "full-grown," in order to be an adequate "body" for such a magnificent, glorious head. So an actual church—like the one in first-century Ephesus, for example, or perhaps the church that you are involved in—might have a lot of growing up to do!

> Ephesians 4:15,16
> … we are to grow up in every way into him who is the head, into Christ, from whom the whole body, joined and held together by every joint with which it is equipped, when each part is working properly, makes the body grow so that it builds itself up in love.

For a church to fail to mature, to "grow up," according to the will of God, as the apostle Paul directed, is like some wise guy attaching the *body* of a Michelangelo statue of the "Infant Christ" to the *head* of Michelangelo's "David"! We must do what we can to help the church to which we belong leave immaturity behind. We must not let it become an under-grown, underweight body, seeing that it is attached to that magnificent head, which is Christ's (see Piece #1).

THE PIECES

CHAPTER SIX:
TWENTY-TWO OPINION PIECES

Piece #1: **WHY THERE CAN'T NOT BE A CHURCH**

God has made it very clear that he is absolutely committed to the continuing reality of Christ's people all being grouped together in some specific biblical form of "church-nicity." And here is why.

God has explained in no uncertain terms that the people he has always known, the people who love him and have been called according to his purpose, have had their destinies prearranged [Romans 8:28]. In every case, this "pre-destiny" includes complete conformity to the image of Christ [Romans 8:29]. So says the Word of God. It also makes clear that there is no arriving at this individual destination of Christlikeness without active involvement in an actual church. This is the previously non-debatable fact that now seems to be considered quite optional.

When the apostle Peter (who knew a thing or two about God's intentions for his imperfect, but everlastingly-loved, people) was wrapping up that first letter that became a part of the New Testament, he wrote about his readers being restored, confirmed, strengthened, and established by the God of all grace [1 Peter 5:10]. Who were these readers? Peter described them as "living stones" that were "being built up as a spiritual house… " [1 Peter 2:5].

Now here's the thing. The intention of God to establish and strengthen and confirm and restore each one of his people always has had everything to do with each of them coming to Christ, who is also referred to as "a living stone," and, in fact, is the cornerstone. Every one of God's people, then, is becoming like a stone in a wall of a temple in which God is properly worshipped—worshipped, in fact, by those very living stones, who also are all members of the priesthood of that temple [1 Peter 2:4,5].

At the same time, the Bible makes clear that, while all real believers in Christ are collectively "a temple of God," in which God's Spirit dwells [1 Corinthians 3:16], their own physical bodies are also, each, "a temple of the Holy Spirit" [1 Corinthians 6:19].

And each believer is also a "member" (a body part—perhaps, a pinkie or a kidney or a ductless gland, for example) of the body of Christ [1 Corinthians 12:12]. The head of that body, of course, is Christ himself [Ephesians 4:15,16], who is also the cornerstone of that temple.

In another New Testament metaphor, the church is "the bride of Christ" [Ephesians 5:31,32; Revelation 21:1,2]. But each believer is *not* individually Christ's bride. An individual Christian is not personally destined, according to Ephesians 5, to be full of "splendour, without spot or wrinkle or any such thing… holy and without blemish" [Ephesians 5:27]. Each Christian is an individual body part of the betrothed and beloved bride of Christ (one of her ductless glands or a pinkie or a kidney, perhaps); maybe not perfectly pretty in itself, and not able to accomplish anything much in itself, but still essential to the complete and proper functioning of the body of the bride of Christ, which is the body of Christ, and the temple of God.

But none of this will ever be real in, say, the city in which you live, if all of this does not apply to actual groups of actual people; people who actually live for Christ and regularly assemble to worship God and to serve people, and to love and encourage one another. Only by being an actual church will they properly let "their light," that is, their corporate share of the light of Christ, shine before people [Matthew 5:16; Hebrews 10:24,25; 1 Peter 2:9,10].

So then God really does require every one of his individual "elect exiles" [1 Peter 2:11] to be actually involved in an actual church—so that that particular church is not like a temple with holes in its walls (where certain living stones should be), or like a priesthood (with some of its priests AWOL). Any particular church should not resemble a human body—or a bride—with vital body parts missing.

Therefore, each actual believer must avoid being like a stone that has been brought to life, but is now just lying in a field, or a parking lot, maybe a church parking lot, or a stone that is alive and that breathes and feels and thinks, but doesn't accomplish what God brought it to life, and to that church, to do. In other words, every authentic believer must avoid being like a body part, lying still on a stainless steel shelf in an operating room, all set to be useful to someone, but never actually being transplanted into an actual human body.

Every real church needs some real Christians in order to be "joined and held together by every joint with which it is equipped, when each part is working properly" [Ephesians 4:16]. Every real Christian needs to belong to a real church in which he or she will be restored, confirmed, strengthened, and established by the God of all grace, as God always has intended. And that is why there cannot *not* be a church.

Piece #2: EMOTIONAL SURFER DUDES

I like it when people describe a strong feeling as a "wave of emotion." People speak of waves of joy, waves of anger, waves of fear, and waves of passion. It's a figure of speech that suggests (to me, at least) how we should manage our own emotional lives, such as they are.

Describing a strong emotion as a wave is loaded with significance when combined with a personal knowledge of surfing. I mean, actual surfing with an actual surfboard, on actual waves. (Admittedly, my own knowledge of surfing is second-hand, but my son Ben is a surfer, and I have a number of Beach Boys tunes on my iPod, so I feel I have a basic understanding of the sport.)

What I have come to see is that when I experience a wave of emotion, I have to decide whether to stand up on the surfboard and ride that wave (so to speak), or to lie down on the board and paddle like crazy in the opposite direction. Which of these options is the better choice depends on understanding the sort of wave it is.

A strong wave of desire for something good and right and true should get me up on my board for the ride. And I should try to ride that wave for as long as it lasts, as long as it keeps moving me in a good direction.

On the other hand, if what I am feeling at the moment seems to be taking me to a bad place—the moral equivalent of a rocky shoreline, or a school of sharks, or some particular opportunity to disobey God—then it is very important that I lie low, point my board in the opposite direction, and do my best to paddle hard until each of the waves of that sort are behind me.

When it comes to surfboards, riding is fun and paddling is not much fun at all. But as every experienced surfer dude knows, no wave lasts a long time. And that means that we shouldn't take any wave too seriously, whatever sort of wave it turns out to be. But it's always a good idea to identify the wave of the moment for what it actually is, so as to ride it—or to ignore it—accordingly.

Piece #3: **WITH OR WITHOUT A BIG STICK**

Before there was Bill Watterson's *Calvin and Hobbes* (1985 to 1995), Gary Larson's *The Far Side* (1980 to 1995), and Jim Unger's *Herman* (1975 to 1992), there was Charles M. Schulz's *Peanuts* (1950 to 2000). And so it came about that for Christmas 1969, my 15-year-old self was given a coffee table-sized book of *Peanuts* comic strips. So popular was *Peanuts* in the late 1960's that it wasn't particularly uncool for a young man of my age to happily receive a *Peanuts* book for Christmas. (I'm not kidding—but then, back in the 60's, I was not particularly cool anyway.)

At that point in my life, I was living at home, one of the five children of Ross and Doreen Wilkins. I was the oldest son, and the second oldest child. My older sister and I—just 21 months apart—were, I think, a normal pair of siblings, intermittently sailing into, and then out of, turbulent relational waters.

But shortly after that Christmas, I discovered in that *Peanuts* book a full-page "Sunday comic," featuring another sister and brother duo, Lucy and Linus. That page of simple pen-and-ink drawings permanently changed my relationship with my sister Jane. And it has also helped me in many other relational experiences ever since. For all the years I was a pastor in London, that particular comic strip was framed, and hanging on a wall in my office—for all to see, and for me to keep in mind. Here's the gist of it.

Lucy notices her younger brother Linus building a snowman. She walks over to him and asks, "What would you do if I pushed your snowman over?"

Linus pauses a moment, and then answers her. "Nothing...what *could* I do? You're bigger and stronger than I am... You're older... you can run faster... I really couldn't do anything to stop you..." He goes on to make a few additional remarks in the same vein, all of them spoken in the same calm, quiet tone. Lucy thinks for a moment, and then simply walks away. Linus returns to his snowman work. And he says to himself, "Little by little I'm becoming an expert at the soft answer."

To me, on the one hand, what Linus said was just funny, as *Peanuts* always was to me in those days. On the other hand, Linus's behaviour was another example of why he had always been my favourite *Peanuts'* character. But on top of that, that punch line came to me as a whole new idea about getting along with people I sometimes did not get along with. A soft answer. I made up my mind to remember that concept.

It was fully two or three years later, when I was 17 or 18, and just beginning to take the Bible seriously, that I discovered that Linus's "soft answer" came from the Old Testament.

> Proverbs 15:1
> A soft answer turneth away wrath: but grievous words stir up anger. (KJV)

This Piece is intended to record that that Bible verse (and Linus's use of it) travelled with me into my pastoring years. It gave me a clear understanding that my challenging personal interactions will generally go in one of two ways, depending on whether I resort to "grievous words," or I respond "softly."

It was the American president Theodore Roosevelt who, in the year 1900, made famous the phrase, "Speak softly and carry a big stick." He was referring to U.S. foreign policy, I think. But I have learned that whatever I happen to be carrying at any given time, in my arms, on my shoulders, or in my heart, a soft answer remains, almost always, the very best sort of answer.

Piece #4: NO WAITING?

In what we think of, and refer to, as his second letter (although he probably wrote more than two in his lifetime), the apostle Peter reflected on a mind-boggling night he spent with two friends, who happened to be brothers, on the top of a hill, in the company of the Man who had permanently interrupted their lives. "We were eyewitnesses of his majesty," Peter wrote. "For when he received honour and glory from God the Father, and the voice was borne to him by the Majestic Glory, 'This is my beloved Son, with whom I am well pleased,' we ourselves heard this very voice borne from heaven, for we were with him on the holy mountain" [2 Peter 1:17,18].

Reading on, we find that Peter made mention of that staggeringly memorable night for the purpose of comparison. Then he shocks us who are reading his letter carefully by stating that *that* mountain-top experience—in which Christ was visibly glorified, and in which God the Father spoke to them audibly!—did not surpass all other experiences in its power to convince Peter and his friends of the reality of Christ's claims. Peter explained, "We have <u>something more sure</u>, the prophetic word" [2 Peter 1:19].

This we could call a striking—even shocking—comparison. The words of the prophets are considered more sure, more authenticating, than a personal vision of Jesus Christ in all his glory? No wonder that Peter urged his readers to pay attention to the prophecies; to give the prophecies our intense, undivided attention "as to <u>a lamp shining in a dark place, until the day dawns and the morning star rises in your hearts</u>" [2 Peter 1:19].

Having said that, Peter explained how the prophetic writings came about. "No prophecy was ever produced by the will of man," he stated, "but men spoke from God as they were carried along by the Holy Spirit" [2 Peter 1:21]. Peter understood these writings of the prophets to be of miraculous origin—and more miraculous, or miraculous in a more enlightening way, than that spectacular incident on "the holy mountain." If we can see that his perspective is different than ours regarding the relative value of personal spiritual experience, we can probably say the same thing about Peter's view of the experience of becoming a Christian. These days, well-run evangelistic organizations often "work their stuff" in such a way that no waiting for salvation is necessary. The common thinking is that it requires no more time to become a committed Christian than the few seconds it takes to raise one hand, or check a box on the card provided. But Peter seemed *to expect* a waiting period.

Let's read it again.

> 2 Peter 1:19,20
> And we have the prophetic word more fully confirmed, to which you will do well to <u>pay attention</u> as to a lamp shining in a dark place, <u>until the day dawns and the morning star rises in your hearts</u>, knowing this first of all, that no prophecy of Scripture comes from someone's own interpretation.

Peter wrote as if he *expected* a waiting period in the experience of "seeing the light," that is, the experience of truly grasping the gospel truths of who Jesus is, and of what Jesus has accomplished for all who commit themselves to him. My thought is that this one idea explains a lot; specifically a lot about our own methods and expectations of leading people to Christ, and the results that often follow.

If the apostles *expected* a waiting period between the experience of "the lights going on," and the making of a lifelong commitment to Jesus Christ, then we should too. There might be many people among us who have avoided the inconvenience or annoyance or humiliation of "waiting upon the Lord" by simply assuming that they have already received whatever it is that the Lord is handing out to applicants. That's my thought.

My corresponding question is: Does any of this explain the present anemic state of Christianity in our part of the world in these days? I once heard J.I. Packer say something about the church in North America being 3,000 miles wide and a half an inch deep. So, why so shallow?

Piece #5: A BOX OF LITTLE STICKS

A guy I know quite well, and respect and like a lot, asked me a question a while ago. He wanted to know about a decision I had made as the pastor of the church. He asked me his question, and then apologized for questioning me at all. I explained my reasons as well as I could, acknowledging that the decision I made was a judgment call, and that I understood why my decision might be questioned. And then I went back to his apology.

"You didn't need to apologize," I told him. And then I surprised him by adding, "In fact, you should have apologized if you *hadn't* questioned me." This he asked me to explain—so I proceeded to.

Making decisions is what leaders do, and some of their decisions are bound to raise questions. A leader needs to be able to answer these questions, but he can't if they are never asked. When a person with a question chooses not to ask it, that question becomes like a little stick that goes into a box and gets carried around—perhaps for years. The question might be about a little thing, but like other little sticks, it goes into a box and stays there. If the holder of the box keeps choosing not to ask the leader the questions that his actions raise, the box can get quite full. This, I think, explains what was the only horrible part of my work as a pastor.

The only horrible part of my work as a pastor was the experience of entirely losing the respect and confidence of some previously-enthusiastic and supportive church member. Such a complete change of mind about my ability to lead, or about my integrity, or about my intelligence, or all three, sometimes seemed to me to come about suddenly. But I am quite sure that was never how it happened. Rather, the sudden change of heart was the eventual outcome of a number of disappointments, perceptions of failure, suspicions about motives—and un-asked questions. Then, as the old campfire song goes, "it only takes a spark to get a fire going."

> James 3:6
> The tongue is a fire, a world of unrighteousness. The tongue is set among our members, staining the whole body, setting on fire the entire course of life, and set on fire by hell.

So I thanked my faithful friend for caring enough to ask me about that decision he couldn't make sense of. And I encouraged him not only to feel free to do the same the next time, but to feel obligated to do so, as an indication that he values our relationship, just as I do.

Piece #6:   HARD TO BELIEVE

It is plainly written that the first disciples had a hard time believing that the resurrection of Christ had actually happened.

> Mark 16:9-11
> ... [Jesus] appeared first to Mary Magdalene, from whom he had cast out seven demons. She went and told those who had been with him, as they mourned and wept. But when they heard that he was alive and had been seen by her, <u>they would not believe it</u>.

Happily, in due time, those first disciples did believe it. With all their hearts. Peter, for example. Since the original eye-witnesses had a hard time grasping the facts, I suppose we can be excused for sometimes suffering from the same incredulity. But it *is* a problem, and a big deal, because ever so much depends on believing in the Lord, and in what the Bible tells us about him. Paul the apostle affirmed:

> Romans 10:9
> … if you confess with your mouth that Jesus is Lord and <u>believe in your heart that God raised him from the dead</u>, you will be saved.

So then, what are we to do with the things we find hard to believe? I have a couple of suggestions.

a) *Get over it!*

All kinds of true things are hard to believe! In fact, almost every true thing is! For example:

1. *The speed of the earth around the sun.*

   Evidently the earth is moving around the Sun in a circle that has a radius of about 150,000,000 kilometers—and it is moving fast! How fast? Fast enough to complete one orbit of 940,000,000 kilometers in just 365¼ days. That is, 110,000 kilometers an hour; which is 30 kilometers per second. This is what we have been told. This planet we live on is orbiting that fast. And we all believe it.

2. *How a baby is born.*

   In this case, every detail is hard to believe—but I have been an actual eye-witness. More than once. In fact, for the births of two of my three children, I remained fully conscious for the entire process. The first time I saw one of our babies emerge from its mother's body, I was hardly able to believe what I was seeing. But I *was* seeing it with my own eyes. So I believed that it really did happen, and I still do.

3. Etc.

   All kinds of other unbelievable things are true. How our eyes see, how our ears hear, how birds migrate, how birds make nests, how spiders spin webs, how spiders even think to spin webs—ever so many things are beyond our comprehension. And then there's photosynthesis, and nuclear fusion, and solar eclipses, and gravity. We believe all kinds of things that are unbelievable. So we need to get over this tendency to be bothered that we find something "hard to believe."

b) *Get on with it!*

Believe the earth is travelling very very fast. Believe that babies are born by being pushed out of their mothers' bodies. And believe the good news that Jesus Christ has risen from the dead. While you are at it, believe the other essential details of the gospel, the good news of salvation through faith in Jesus Christ, as it is explained in the Bible. Of course, it is all hard to believe! Every true thing is!

Piece #7:   FRUITLESS QUESTIONS

When things go terribly wrong for a Christian—I mean, a believer in Christ who takes seriously his Lord's standards of discipleship—an obvious question to ask is "Why?"—meaning, "Why has this bad prognosis, or this business reversal, or this ugly divorce, or this disastrous vacation, or this ridiculous car accident, or this death of a loved one, or this unfathomable veterinarian bill, happened to me?" Or more lyrically, "Why do these 'sorrows like sea billows roll'"?

The author of the Book of Hebrews served up a detailed answer to all variations of this question, borrowing freely from the Book of Proverbs to do so [Proverbs 3:11,12]. In Hebrews 12, we can see five distinct elements of the answer to such questions.

FIVE EXPLANATIONS FOR A BAD THING THAT JUST HAPPENED

1. *This "discipline" is God's loving and fatherly "child-training"*

   In these Bible verses, the word "discipline" means, most plainly, a parent's training of his (or her) child. In the Greek New Testament, the word translated "discipline" is based on the word for "young child."

   Hebrews 12:5–11
   And have you forgotten the exhortation that addresses you as sons? "My son, do not regard lightly the discipline of the Lord, nor be weary when reproved by him. For the Lord disciplines the one he loves, and chastises every son whom he receives." It is for discipline that you have to endure. God is treating you as sons. For what son is there whom his father does not discipline? If you are left without discipline, in which all have participated, then you are illegitimate children and not sons. Besides this, we have had earthly fathers who disciplined us and we respected them. Shall we not much more be subject to the Father of spirits and live? For they disciplined us for a short time as it seemed best to them, but he disciplines us for our good, that we may share his holiness. For the moment all discipline seems painful rather than pleasant, but later it yields the peaceful fruit of righteousness to those who have been trained by it.

2. This *"discipline... painful rather than pleasant"*—*"for the moment"*—some time *"later,"* will produce *"the peaceful fruit of righteousness"* [Hebrews 12:11].

> So we are talking about God's plan of "short-term pain for long-term gain." Just like medicine that tastes terrible, but is terribly good for you.

3. *Under some circumstances, this "discipline" is God's response to our bad behaviour.*

> What kind of parent sees his child doing something dangerous (with a screw driver and an electrical outlet, for example) and does not intervene???
>
> Proverbs 13:24
> Whoever spares the rod hates their children, but <u>the one who loves</u> their children is <u>careful to discipline.</u>

4. *Sometimes, this "discipline" is God's response to our potential for bearing more good fruit.*

> John 15:1,2
> I am the true vine, and my Father is the vinedresser. Every branch in me that does not bear fruit he takes away, and every branch that <u>does bear fruit</u> he prunes, that it may <u>bear more fruit.</u>

5. *Always, the "discipline of the Lord" is God's reason for the difficult details of our lives as he continues to conform us to the likeness of his one "non-adopted" Son.*

> 2 Corinthians 4:16–18
> So we do not lose heart. Though our outer self is wasting away, our inner self is being renewed

day by day. For <u>this light momentary affliction is preparing for us an eternal weight of glory beyond all comparison</u>, as we look not to the things that are seen but to the things that are unseen. For the things that are seen are transient, but the things that are unseen are eternal.

Piece #8: EVERYTHING CONNECTS

In the small eastern Ontario city where I lived in the early 1970's, there was a department store called Towers. In view of the possibility that anyone wonders what happened to it, the fact is that all 51 Towers stores were purchased in 1990 by Zellers. So say the wizards of Wikipedia. At any rate, Towers department stores were swallowed alive, and are now gone from the world.

I will now get to the point. Before they disappeared, Towers advertised with a slogan which, strangely and annoyingly, I still remember 45 years later. It was a jingle, and regretfully, I also still remember the tune. Here are the lyrics:

> At Towers, everything connects. The last day of
> one sale is the first day of the next.

I have one favorable thing to say about the historical reality of Towers department stores. Their slogan was correct. That is why I came to think it is a good and profitable idea to develop a talent for walking past a candy dish, or a plate of cookies, without indulging.

For many years, there *was* a small dish of Scotch mints, situated on a book shelf immediately outside my church office door. My faithful and hard-working secretary had placed it there, and kept it filled, in the hopes that people coming to see us would be sweet in disposition and pleasant in speech.

The philosophy I developed in my years in that office is that there was greater value in resisting the urge to pop into my mouth a tasty little piece of sugar than to just go ahead and take one. On principle. The value of resisting came from the fact that, when it comes to living a disciplined life, or more generally, an obedient life, Towers was right. Everything connects—and therefore the last moment of one battle, or binge, is the first moment of the next.

What I mean is that I've learned that developing and maintaining a discipline of some sort—practically of any sort—has an influence on other areas of life that require self-discipline. The opposite is also the case. Slackness, sloppiness and a lack of self-control are also contagious. And so a little bowl of candies *can* serve a person well as an opportunity to practice saying "No" to the urges and appetites and desires of our humanity.

Fitting with this is what A. W. Tozer once said, I think. (Who knows how many things that we think were said by a famous person actually were said?) See the 19th Bit. At any rate, it is thought that the world's only famous Alliance pastor once answered the question of how long a person should fast. I have been told he answered, "As long as it takes to show your stomach that *it* is not in charge." If he did say that, I agree with him. And if he didn't, I think he would have wished that he had.

Piece #9: "HAVEN'T YOU ALREADY READ THAT?"

A question I am accustomed to being asked is why I read some books over and over again, for example, *The Wind in the Willows, Out of the Silent Planet, That Hideous Strength, Till We Have Faces, The Lord of the Rings* and *The Everlasting Man*. I answer, "It's about vision."

One thing I have picked up over the years is that maintaining a vision for personal godliness requires, and deserves, effort. Those six books I have read over and over again because they each remind me, over and over again, of the sort of man I am committed to becoming—and remaining.

Reading *The Lord of the Rings* over and over again, for example, refreshes my vision of humility, perseverance and a pure heart—mostly because of Aragorn and Faramir and Frodo and Sam (in the books, *not* the movies).

Reading *The Wind in the Willows* over and over again reminds me, because of Rat, of how kind and understanding and cheerful and unselfish a friend can be. And Toad reminds me of how infuriating a friend can be.

Reading *The Everlasting Man* over and over again reminds me of how good and right and appropriate and exhilarating it is to believe and worship and love and serve Jesus Christ.

That's what I say to explain. And if the person who asked the question is still listening, I sometimes go on to say that while the books don't change in between my reading of them, I do. Maintaining some visions is hard work—and important.

Additionally, I might add that these great books are all deep and detailed and complicated enough that, even after twenty or thirty readings, I continue to stumble upon details of which I have no recollection. Maybe this shows that I'm actually not a very smart person. Maybe that is exactly why some people ask me that question.

Piece #10: EXPLANATIONS FOR A DEATH-BED CONVERSION

I once watched Christopher Hitchens, a famous atheist, in a televised interview. He was talking of his nasty case of cancer, and the chemotherapy he was receiving, and the question of whether or not his terminal illness had changed, or ever would change, his ideas about God. Mr. Hitchens admitted the possibility of a death-bed conversion, but assured the interviewer that if that *were* to happen, it could only be attributed to one of two things: the delirious effect of the pain-killing medication, or insanity caused by his pain and suffering.

History however reveals that there is a third possible explanation. Paul the apostle wrote in the second letter to the Corinthians (4:6) that sometimes, the "God, who said, 'Let light shine out of darkness,' [also shines in human] hearts to give the light of the knowledge of the glory of God in the face of Jesus Christ." It *has* happened. In fact, it has happened a lot. And it has happened to some equally antagonistic non-Christians who were quite obviously as intelligent and educated as Mr. Hitchens.

It happened to the apostle Paul himself in fact [Acts 9:1-9], and to Augustine and Pascal and T.S. Eliot and C.S. Lewis—and, of course, to hundreds of millions of men and women and children who did not go on to live lives, or to write writings, for which they are remembered to this day. Each one would say that the motive power, in his case, was the grace of the Lord Jesus Christ. And so the hearts of many an angry antagonist are changed.

In regard to the unbelief of the people we love, we should pray for such an amazing work of grace—and watch for it. Paul, the angry-opponent-turned-apostle-and-preacher was speaking from experience when he wrote that the gospel is "the power of God for salvation to everyone who believes" [Romans 1:16].

> Malachi 4:2
> The sun of righteousness shall rise with healing in its wings.
>
> John 1:4,5
> In [Christ is] life, and the life [is] the light of the world. The light shines in the darkness, and the darkness has not overcome it.

Piece #11: THANKING SOMEONE

Canada's Thanksgiving Day has only been an annual event since 1879 when the still-quite-new Canadian government made it so. It was following the example of the United States of America. Fourteen years earlier, President Lincoln declared Thanksgiving Day a yearly holiday. So, compared to Christmas and Easter, it's all still quite new. But harvest festivals have been celebrated in North America off and on since 1556 when the first governor of Florida enjoyed a happy meal at the beach with the local inhabitants.

Harvest is a natural thing to celebrate, and it is almost as natural to bring a sense of gratitude to the feast. But this second impulse raises questions. Who is it we are thanking? Is there any sense in saying "Thanks" at all without someone to say it *to*?

Certainly, there are many things to be thankful for. The spring sunshine that thawed the soil that warmed the seeds, and the summer sunshine that kept the plants photosynthesizing without scorching them, and the rain that fell to water the plants, and did not drown them. Is it these lifeless things we should thank?

To many people, the idea of an undirected expression of appreciation just won't do; like a thank-you note mailed in an unaddressed envelope. Many people are too personally involved with the things of the world to keep things so impersonal. And so, many people have learned to follow the instructions.

> Psalm 100:3–5
> Know that the LORD, he is God! It is he who made
> us, and we are his; we are his people, and the sheep
> of his pasture. Enter his gates with thanksgiving,
> and his courts with praise! Give thanks to him;
> bless his name! For the LORD is good; his steadfast

love endures forever, and his faithfulness to all generations.

Piece #12: NOT EVERYONE WHO SOUNDS ARROGANT

"You know what I dislike about you Christians the most?" he asked.

"No," I replied.

"Your arrogance!" he said.

It sounded like the start of an interesting conversation, so I did my best to seem humble and lovable. "Arrogance? What do you mean?"

"What I mean is that you Christians think you are the only ones in the world who are right about everything, and that everyone else in the world is completely wrong! That's arrogant!"

"It does sound arrogant," I replied. "But I think you're mistaking us for somebody else. It's not the Christians who think everyone else is completely wrong." He didn't turn away and he didn't seem to be getting angry, so I kept going. "Christians are the people who have committed themselves to Jesus Christ. They do so because they believe he is the only begotten Son of God. Believing that, they also believe that he was speaking the truth when he said, 'I am the way, the truth and the life.' With unambiguous statements like that to think about, it seems to me pretty obvious that Christ was either telling the truth or he wasn't. We Christians are the people who believe he *was* telling the truth."

"But you don't believe that everyone else is wrong?"

"Well, not completely wrong. For example, we Christians think that Jews and Muslims are right when they say that there is only one God. And on that point, they think we're right, too. It's the atheists who think that they are the only ones who have it right and that everyone else in the world (that is, anyone who thinks that any sort of God exists) is completely wrong."

"So you don't think Christians are arrogant?"

"Well, not all of us! And if we *are*, it's not because of what we think about the claims of Christ. For that matter, believing the claims of Christ and committing oneself to him involves a pretty major dose of humility. The offer Jesus made was to forgive and to cleanse and to lead. Signing up for that requires some sort of admission that we are guilty, defiled and lost—a pretty humbling experience!"

I thought I would close things off before he changed the subject for me, so I turned to leave. And then, with what I hoped was a disarming smile, I concluded. "Considering what it really means to be a follower of Christ, an arrogant Christian is actually a contradiction in terms."

Piece #13: ABOLISHING HEARTS AND MINDS

A while ago, I read what a blogger blogged about C.S. Lewis: that while it is more popular than ever, and in fact, very hip, to be known as "a big C. S. Lewis fan," in truth there is very little reading of C.S. Lewis actually going on.

At the risk of seeming to be simply bragging that I *do* read a lot of Lewis, I hereby weigh in with the humble opinion that what a great majority of "C.S. Lewis fans" base their enthusiasm upon are the Narnia movies—or the excellent "Focus on the Family" audio recordings of the actual texts of the Narnia books—and in some advanced cases, some reading of *Mere Christianity* or *The Screwtape Letters*.

To honour the memory of the man himself, and of the significance of his literary works, I hereby extol the virtues of one of the lesser-known (if ever actually read) writings of Lewis: his short and profound book entitled *The Abolition of Man*; subtitled *Reflections on education with special reference to the teaching of English in the upper forms of schools.* My reason for doing so is my opinion that its theme—which, by the way, he also featured two years later in his brilliant novel *That Hideous Strength*—is an explanation of one of the primary factors responsible for the rarity of the actual reading of any books.

This Piece is also about the collapse of our education system and the rise of what has often been grandly referred to as "postmodernism." *The Abolition of Man* is Lewis's attempt to rescue what he calls "the doctrine of objective value." In the first of its three short chapters, he writes of the pressing need that he saw (in the early 1940's!) to "transmit manhood to men." (Shocking language for our times. So politically incorrect! So gender-specific!)

The first chapter is entitled "Men without Chests," by which he means human beings who have lost, or who have never developed, a heart to love with great intensity the virtuous actions and wise words of good people, and to despise with great hatred the evil actions and foolish words of evil people. Lewis ends the first chapter (and entices us into reading the other two) with this brilliant and stirring summary of the horrible results of being "chestless."

> Such is the tragi-comedy of our situation—we continue to clamor for those very qualities we are rendering impossible. You can hardly open a periodical without coming across the statement that what our civilization needs is more 'drive', or dynamism, or self-sacrifice, or 'creativity.' In a sort of ghastly simplicity we remove the organ and demand the function. We make men without chests and expect of them virtue and enterprise. We laugh at honour and are shocked to find traitors in our midst. We castrate and bid the geldings be fruitful.

For my part, and at the risk of sounding like one more illiterate book-skimmer, I say, "I am on *that* man's side. I want to buy what *that* man is selling!" In actual fact, he's not selling anything anymore—or writing anymore. It is a tragedy of the 20th century that CSL died at the age of just 64. I shudder to think of the number of books by him that are unavailable to all of us because he died before writing them. But he did write quite a few great books, and most of them are still in print. "Being dead, he still speaks"—to all who will actually read them.

Piece #14: THREE DEAD MEN ON HAPPINESS

Here are three interrelated thoughts from three of my Dead Men, who, if given the opportunity, would have disagreed with each other profoundly on many important topics (for example, "free will"), but who would have agreed with each other on the subject of happiness.

G.K. Chesterton (1874-1936) wrote of the futile quest for happiness of the "pessimistic pleasure-seeker" as "taught by the very powerful and very desolate philosophy of Oscar Wilde. It is the *carpe diem* religion; but the *carpe diem* religion is not the religion of happy people, but of very unhappy people. Great joy does not gather the rosebuds while it may; its eyes are fixed on the immortal rose which Dante saw." Chesterton is being very helpful here by raising the notion that happiness is not going to happen if it is pursued for its own sake, but rather only when some immortal thing is envisioned and focused upon. So as for our everyday wishes for happiness, let us take note that the best way to achieve it is not to make happiness our goal.

Jonathan Edwards (1703-1758) wrote more explicitly, although just as poetically, about what that "immortal thing" actually is:

> The enjoyment of God is the only happiness with which our souls can be satisfied ... Fully to enjoy

> God is infinitely better than the most pleasant accommodations here. Fathers and mothers, husbands, wives, or children, or the company of earthly friends, are but shadows; but God is the substance. These are but scattered beams, but God is the sun. These are but streams. But God is the ocean.

Edwards said it. I believe it. And from experience, I have learned that my happiness is best encountered when my highest goal is God himself—and when the challenge to which I am paying attention is the "upward call of God in Christ Jesus" [Philippians 3:14].

C.S. Lewis (1898-1963) wrote, also poetically and plainly and helpfully, "God designed the human machine to run on Himself. He is the fuel our spirits were designed to burn."

From the pens (or a quill) of two or three witnesses shall every word be established.

Piece #15: THE COMPLICATED MATTER OF "FREE WILL"

Anyone who wants to discuss "free will" should begin by explaining what he or she means by "will"—and what sort of "freedom" he or she is meaning to discuss. Here's what I mean by the will and human freedom.

The "will" is our human capacity to *prefer* something, and to take action in the power of that preference. The concept of "free will" is complicated because, actually, and historically, and in the future, the "will" is "free" in four distinct, and non-compatible ways. Every human at every moment of his life, has one, but only one, particular sort of "free will." This fourfold diversity arises from humanity's four different moral conditions.[15]

CONDITION ONE: HUMANITY IN EDEN

According to the Bible, human beings lived first in a state of freedom.

- Free *from* sin [Genesis 1:27]
- Free to refrain from sin [Genesis 2:16,17]
- Free *to* sin [Genesis 3:6]

Those were the days! But then began humanity's disaster, and its disastrous new relationship to sin.

CONDITION TWO: HUMANITY IN SIN

Human beings were different once they had sinned. So was their experience regarding "free will".

- *Not* free to refrain from sin: *a slave to sin, dead in sins* [John 8:34; Ephesians 2:1]
- Free *to* sin (As a skydiver is said to be in "free fall") [Ephesians 2:2,3]
- Free *from* righteousness [Romans 6:20]

---

15 These four conditions of humanity I learned from Arthur C. Custance, in his book "The Sovereignty of Grace" (Available at custance.org.) The same perspective is presented in Chapter IX of the Westminster Confession of Faith, and is expounded in "Human Nature in Its Fourfold State," by Thomas Boston, a Scottish Puritan minister.

It wasn't called the Fall for nothing. And that would have been humanity's doom, except for Christ, who said, "If the Son sets you free, you are free indeed!" [John 8:36]

CONDITION THREE: HUMANITY IN CHRIST

In this condition, the human moral condition makes everything complicated.

- Free from sin's penalty [John 8:36; Romans 8:1]
- *Not* free to sin, *sort of*: *a slave to Christ* [Romans 6:17,18]
- Free to refrain from sin, *sort of*. In this moral state, it takes determination, and the help of the Holy Spirit, to remain free [Galatians 5:1,13,16]

CONDITION FOUR: HUMANITY IN GLORY

There *will be* a fourth moral state, once "he who began a good work in [us]" brings it to completion [Philippians 1:6].

- Free from sin, period [1 John 3:2; 1 Corinthians 15:49-57]

EXTRA PARAGRAPH TO EXPLAIN IMPLICATIONS OF CONDITION THREE

The details of "man's free will" are so complicated that "free will" is a term too unhelpful to be useful. In the terms of the 33rd Bit, it is not the idea of our own "free will" that we should be gripping tightly while we also grip tightly "God's sovereignty." It is our "moral responsibility" we should be gripping. One of the great stopping points in our ascent of the mountain of the knowledge of God (see the 24th Bit) is the place where we ask, how can God hold us responsible for our moral choices while he exercises sovereign control over all things?

Another approach to the same point on the mountain is to ask, how can God *justly* hold us responsible for our moral choices if we are either slaves to sin or slaves to righteousness? (See the 11th Bit.) The best answer, in the opinion of some theologians at least, is found in an understanding of the nature of human enslavement to sin, or to righteousness. And for my money (but it's actually free online), the best explanation of this comes from Jonathan Edwards in a treatise he called, "On the Freedom of the Will," especially "Part I. Section IV. Of the distinction of <u>natural</u> and <u>moral</u> necessity, and <u>inability</u>." The entire treatise, and other works of Jonathan Edwards, can be found at various sites on the Internet.

Piece #16: CAREFULLY, NOT QUICKLY

"The words of the Lord are pure words, like silver refined in a furnace on the ground, purified seven times." This we read in Psalm 12:6. And someone might ask, "How pure is *that?*" In Proverbs, something similar is stated. "Every word of God is true" [30:5]. And someone might ask, "*How* true?" The Word of God is *so* pure and *so* true that it matters that we who read the Bible read it carefully, and that we carefully notice the details of what we read so that we see in what way the New Testament writers (and "New Testament speakers") quote statements in the Old Testament.

Take Paul the apostle as an example. To explain that God's promises to Abraham about his "seed" referred particularly to Christ, Paul wrote:

> Galatians 3:16
> Now the promises were made to Abraham and to his <u>offspring</u>. It does not say, "And to <u>offsprings</u>," referring to many, but referring to one, "And to your <u>offspring</u>," who is Christ.

The apostle's argument rests entirely on the fact that the noun is singular rather than plural ("offspring" and "offsprings" can be translated more plainly as "seed" and "seeds").

For the similar approach of the "New Testament speakers," we can look to Jesus, who in defending the truth of the resurrection of the body, said to the Sadducees:

> Matthew 22:31,32
> And as for the resurrection of the dead, have you not read what was said to you by God: "I am the God of Abraham, and the God of Isaac, and the God of Jacob"? He is not God of the dead, but of the living."

Here, the Lord's argument rests on the use of the present tense, "am," rather than the past tense, "was," in Exodus 3:6.

In both of these cases, the argument is based entirely on a very particular detail of one biblical text, as if the exact details of every biblical statement ("every jot and tittle") are sufficiently trustworthy to be used in these precise ways. It is as if the words of the Lord are *pure* words. As if every word of God is *true*. And as if the Bible is not a collection of writings intended for browsing, or skimming, or speed-reading. "The words of the Lord *are* pure words, like silver refined in a furnace on the ground, purified seven times" [Psalm 12:6]. When it is the Bible we are reading, let us read carefully.

Piece #17: ASSUMING NORMAL

Maybe it's the peculiar period of history in which we are living, or maybe it's the faulty way in which we were raised and educated. Maybe it's the number of Participation Trophies we were awarded. But it seems to me to be often the case that a person enters adulthood with an excessive view of his or her own general importance and overall excellence.

Only hoping to be helpful, I hereby encourage readers to protect themselves from the potential harms that result from such rampant self-esteem, and from failing to assume that we are normal rather than above (or even far above) average; that we are in fact, for the most part, ordinary, not extraordinary, human beings; that we can't always accomplish anything whatsoever that we set our hearts on, as so many valedictorians declare; that God does not in fact think that each one of us is altogether awesome, as some authors and pastors insist.

I am in favour of us all holding to humble convictions about our worth; and maintaining these convictions steadfastly until circumstances strongly suggest otherwise. To do so can be a great liberation. There is freedom in learning to see yourself as a "regular" guy (or girl); a person who is energized, mobilized, empowered and exhilarated by a reasonable set of expectations and the realistic hope of living an honest, competent and productive human life.

All of this fits with the counseling strategy I adopted over my years of attempting to help troubled people. I sometimes encouraged them to set aside, at least for the moment, all the complicated solutions to personal and interpersonal challenges and problems, pursuing instead the simple solutions that the situation suggests.

"Let's assume you are normal," I would say to people. "For the time being, I mean."

And then I would take the time to ask the troubled person if he or she is eating and sleeping well, and exercising regularly, and if he or she is intentionally associating with happy, healthy people at least some of the time, and if he or she is keeping busy working at something worthwhile. All of these things, and some others besides, are the component parts of a normal human life. They are the basic building blocks of the happy, peaceful life of a normal person. But such building blocks can evade the grasp of a person who for one reason or another assumes himself (or herself) to be someone really quite extraordinary.

Piece #18:   **ONLY IN CHRIST**

No wonder that we people, when we pray, usually end the prayer, whether in a public setting or a small group, with the words, "in the name of Jesus." The New Testament is so very detailed in its explanation that every privilege, every blessing, every part of God's redemption of us, is ours "in Christ," which is to say, Christ alone qualifies us to be so kindly treated by God. This is the note upon which the apostle Paul begins his mighty letter to the "faithful saints" living in first-century Ephesus.

> Ephesians 1:3–14
> Blessed be the God and Father of our Lord Jesus Christ, who has blessed us <u>in Christ</u> with every spiritual blessing in the heavenly places, even as he chose us <u>in him</u> before the foundation of the world, that we should be holy and blameless before him. In love he predestined us for adoption to himself as sons <u>through Jesus Christ</u>, according to the purpose of his will, to the praise of his glorious grace, with which he has blessed us <u>in the Beloved</u>.
>
> <u>In him</u> we have redemption through his blood, the forgiveness of our trespasses, according to the riches of his grace, which he lavished upon us, in all wisdom and insight making known to us the mystery of his will, according to his purpose, which he set forth <u>in Christ</u> as a plan for the fullness of time, to unite all things <u>in him</u>, things in heaven and things on earth.
>
> <u>In him</u> we have obtained an inheritance, having been predestined according to the purpose of him who works all things according to the counsel of his

> will, so that we who were the first to hope <u>in Christ</u> might be to the praise of his glory.
>
> <u>In him</u> you also, when you heard the word of truth, the gospel of your salvation, and believed <u>in him</u>, were sealed with the promised Holy Spirit, who is the guarantee of our inheritance until we acquire possession of it, to the praise of his glory.

Count 'em! Eleven times in twelve verses, Paul the apostle, "as he was carried along by the Holy Spirit" [2 Peter 1:21], plainly stated that the "saints" in Ephesus were blessed by God in many everlasting ways—and all only because they were "in Christ." Being "in Christ" was clearly the most significant detail of the life of each of them. And the same is true for every other "saint," from every other period of history, including our own. We are blessed "with every spiritual blessing in the heavenly places" [vs.3] because we are "in Christ," and were chosen to be, "before the foundation of the world" [vs.4].

" … And we pray all these things in Jesus name." No wonder we hold to this traditional prayer-concluding phrase. It's an acknowledgement of the foundational truth that all we have is ours, and always will be ours, "in Christ." "…As it is written, 'Let the one who boasts, boast in the Lord'" [1 Corinthians 1:31].

Piece #19: **BIBLICAL DIVORCE, AND WHAT COMES NEXT**[16]

There is such a thing as a "biblical divorce" because the word translated "divorce" has, in the Bible, two quite different meanings. On the one hand, "divorce" means the *intentional, sinful destruction* of a marriage through adultery, or desertion, or any other act of covenant breaking—for marriage is a covenant [Malachi 2:14, and also Jeremiah 31:32; Ezekiel 16:8]. It was this "unbiblical" kind of divorce about which the prophet Malachi was prophesying when he wrote of such marriage-destroying sins as "faithlessness," or (in other versions) "treachery" [Malachi 2:13–16].

And it is this sort of divorce that Jesus was speaking out against in the Gospels [Matthew 5:32;19:9; Mark 10:11,12; Luke 16:18].

On the other hand, divorce is, in some circumstances, not a sinful act of faithlessness, but rather *a biblical response to faithlessness*. In other words, there is such a thing as a divorce which is "biblical." (Biblically speaking, divorcing one's faithless spouse is the extreme penalty in a marriage, comparable to excommunication in a church, disinheritance in a family, and execution in a civil state.) It was this sort of divorce that Joseph decided was the "just" thing for a man in his circumstances to do.

> Matthew 1:19
> ... [Mary's] husband, being a just man and unwilling to put her to shame, resolved to divorce her quietly.

---

16 This point of view, and with it, the contents of Piece #20, I learned from R.J. Rushdooney's massive practical commentary on the Ten Commandments, "The Institutes of Biblical Law," and also from Ray Sutton's book "Second Chance." Both are available from Amazon.

Joseph planned to divorce Mary "quietly" because he was "unwilling to put her to shame". But he did resolve to divorce her, in the first place, because he was "a just man". Being a "just man," and misunderstanding Mary's circumstances, he was choosing to do what he thought was the just, or righteous, thing.

The key to understanding this point of view is realizing that all of these serious and important relationships: being married, being a church member, belonging in a family, and being the citizen of a country, are (or at least could, and should, be) covenants, and so highly conditional. So all of these "memberships" are potentially breakable. A solemn exchange of oaths of mutual faithfulness should always be a part of the ceremony with which a covenant begins, as it does (or at least should!) at a wedding, (" ... *for better or worse, for richer or poorer, in sickness and health, and forsaking all others, be faithful only to her [or him]. For as long as you both shall live*").

A "biblical divorce," then, is *a biblical response to faithlessness*. The fact that there *is* such a thing as "biblical remarriage" is strongly and clearly implied in the Book of Deuteronomy. Moses makes clear that there is one sort of remarriage that is not allowed. It "is an abomination before the LORD" to remarry one's own former spouse, after she or he has married someone else, and been divorced by that person [Deuteronomy 24:1-4]. Plainly, if that one specific sort of remarriage is ruled out, it follows that other specific sorts of remarriage are not.

The question of whether or not a divorced person *should* enter into a biblical remarriage is a very serious question, especially if children are still at home. It is certainly a question that warrants godly counsel from wise, biblically-grounded people. Not everything we have a biblical right to do is a good and appropriate thing to do in every circumstance. (See the 31st Bit)

In some cases, the wisest and most godly response to a faithless spouse is to refrain from the biblical option of divorcing the "treacherous" one;

choosing instead to remain in a married state. This is what God did in his covenant relationship with the nation of Israel for many centuries [Jeremiah 3:7]. But he did not refrain endlessly. God waited a very long time, but he did eventually "remarry," this time to a "woman" we know as the "bride of Christ" [Ephesians 5:32].

> Revelation 21:1–4
> Then I saw a new heaven and a new earth, for the first heaven and the first earth had passed away, and the sea was no more. And I saw the holy city, new Jerusalem, coming down out of heaven from God, prepared as <u>a bride adorned for her husband</u>. And I heard a loud voice from the throne saying, "Behold, the dwelling place of God is with man. He will dwell with them, and they will be his people, and God himself will be with them as their God. He will wipe away every tear from their eyes, and death shall be no more, neither shall there be mourning, nor crying, nor pain anymore, for the former things have passed away."

One of the many privileges of being a part of a church is the opportunity it affords to receive godly counsel regarding such difficult questions, from wise people who, preferably, know one or both of the spouses personally. And a church behaving biblically also provides "covenant protection" to the church members afflicted with such a time of personal trial and challenge. Marriage is not without its risks. Being also a "covenant member" of a local church can, and certainly should, be a very helpful source of support to someone finding himself or herself in a marital challenge.

OPINION PIECES

Piece #20: WILD AND UN-TAME WORDS

The previous Piece made reference to the words of Jesus concerning divorce, for example: "Everyone who divorces his wife and marries another commits adultery, and he who marries a woman divorced from her husband commits adultery" [Luke 16:18]. The previous piece was my attempt to explain these strong and dogmatic words. Here is something more to keep in mind about these strong words of Jesus, and the many other strong statements he made.

In reading and studying the Gospel accounts of what our Lord said, we should be aware of the unique nature of his use of language. Jesus had a way of communicating! His words were often startling, even alarming or shocking.

In the Narnia books[17], Mr. Beaver described the mysterious Aslan to the English children, who had not yet met him. "He's wild, you know. Not like a tame lion." C.S. Lewis's point, I think, was inspired by his familiarity with Jesus as he is depicted in the four Gospel accounts. Some of his words, and some of his actions, were, it seems, deliberately "wild" rather than "tame."

In considering his words about divorce, for example in Matthew 5, their context should not be ignored. Immediately before his words on divorce and remarriage (verses 31,32), Jesus spoke on a different subject with wild and un-tame language.

> Matthew 5:29,30
> If your right eye causes you to sin, tear it out and throw it away. For it is better that you lose one of your members than that your whole body be thrown into hell. And if your right hand causes you to sin, cut it off and throw it away. For it is better

---

17 Specifically, "The Lion, the Witch and the Wardrobe"

that you lose one of your members than that your whole body go into hell.

Wild words! Similarly, on other occasions, Jesus spoke of the rich having more difficulty entering the kingdom of God than a camel has going through the eye of a needle [Mark 10:24,25]; that, if people wanted to be disciples of his, they must hate their parents, wife, children and siblings, and renounce everything they own [Luke 14:26, 33]; that his mission in this world was to bring a sword, and not peace [Matthew 10:34]—and to cast fire on the earth and create division [Luke 12:49, 53]. He once told a man whose father had only recently died to "leave the dead to bury their own dead" [Luke 9:60]. And he challenged his antagonists to destroy the temple, assuring them that, when they did, he would rebuild it himself—in just three days [John 2:19]. Such un-tame words!

In view of this "wildness" of the Lion of the tribe of Judah, all the Lord's words must always be considered in the context of the entirety of Scripture. But, of course, every statement in Scripture must be considered in that context. For example, the Old Testament divorce (and remarriage) laws, and the many death penalties, were specifically given by God, through Moses, to God's covenant nation, for Israel had a unique relationship with God in a number of ways. The letters from the apostle Paul and Peter, on the other hand, were written, under the inspiration of the Holy Spirit, to New Testament church leaders and Christian church members regarding practical issues and challenges of life; marriage, for example [1 Corinthians 7:1-40, 1 Peter 3:1-7].

The words of Jesus are the spoken revelation of the One whose name is "the Word of God." He alone is "the King of kings and Lord of lords," from whose "mouth comes a sharp sword" [Revelation 19:13-16].

> 2 Timothy 3:16
> <u>All Scripture</u> is breathed out by God and profitable

for teaching, for reproof, for correction, and for training in righteousness…

Proverbs 30:5
<u>Every word of God</u> proves true; he is a shield to those who take refuge in him.

Psalm 12:6
The words of the LORD are <u>pure words,</u> like silver refined in a furnace on the ground, purified seven times.

Piece #21: FORGIVENESS, CONDITIONAL AND OTHERWISE

Just as there are two kinds of divorce (See Piece #19), so there are, in the Bible, two kinds of forgiveness. Just like divorce, forgiveness is a *complicated* thing.

One kind of forgiveness can be called "<u>unconditional</u>," because it does not require any specific behaviour, or even any specific attitude, from the offending person. Regardless of the condition of our relationship to the person who has wronged us, and even irrespective of that person's attitude towards us, in some circumstances the most expedient thing for us to do might be simply to "forgive" that evildoer. But what does that sort of forgiveness actually mean? I think it means to "let go" of the hatred, to decide to give the whole matter to God, and to begin to give it as little of your attention as possible. This is an action we can take by which "no root of bitterness springs up and causes trouble, and by it many become defiled." In some circumstances, holding on to bitterness and hatred, even when such feelings are justified, will mean "fail[ing] to obtain the grace of God" [Hebrews 12:15], for to hold on to bitter and hateful feelings is to refuse to obey the instructions of God given to us through the apostle Paul.

> Romans 12:16–21
> Live in harmony with one another. Do not be haughty, but associate with the lowly. Never be wise in your own sight. <u>Repay no one evil for evil</u>, but give thought to do what is honorable in the sight of all. If possible, <u>so far as it depends on you, live peaceably with all</u>. Beloved, <u>never avenge yourselves, but leave it to the wrath of God</u>, for it is written, "Vengeance is mine, I will repay, says the Lord." To the contrary, "if your enemy is hungry, feed him; if he is thirsty, give him something to drink; for by so doing you will heap burning coals on his head." <u>Do not be overcome by evil, but overcome evil with good</u>.

Immediately following these words of Paul regarding overcoming evil done to a person, he writes:

> Romans 13:1-4
> Let every person be subject to the governing authorities. For there is no authority except from God, and those that exist have been instituted by God. Therefore whoever resists the authorities resists what God has appointed, and those who resist will incur judgment. For rulers are not a terror to good conduct, but to bad. Would you have no fear of the one who is in authority? Then do what is good, and you will receive his approval, for he is God's servant for your good. But if you do wrong, be afraid, for he does not bear the sword in vain. For he is the servant of God, an avenger who carries out God's wrath on the wrongdoer.

Often, because the first six verses in this quotation are in Chapter 12, and the remaining four verses are in the following chapter, the logical connection between these 10 verses escapes the attention of many. But what some of those people would be greatly helped to know is that the God-given practical application of the instructions to "leave [vengeance] to the wrath of God," and to "overcome evil with good," is to "be subject to the governing authorities," which in some cases simply means to "call the cops." In almost no cases, do these verses mean that we should keep to ourselves the evil deed done to us. The God-ordained civil authority protects us (and our neighbours!) from evildoers. "Just forgiving" the evil done to you can add up to protecting the evildoer from the law, and so helping the evildoer to conceal his crimes, and to remain at large in the neighborhood. Doing so would be, in a small way at least, to become partially to blame for the harm done to his next victim.

On the other hand, there is another kind of forgiveness which is "conditional." It is the forgiveness that is patterned on God's forgiveness of us.

> Colossians 3:12,13
> Put on then, as God's chosen ones, holy and
> beloved, compassionate hearts, kindness, humility,
> meekness, and patience, bearing with one another
> and, if one has a complaint against another,
> forgiving each other; as the Lord has forgiven you,
> so you also must forgive.

> 1 John 1:8,9
> If we confess our sins, [God] is faithful and just
> to forgive us our sins and to cleanse us from all
> unrighteousness.

In my days of pastoral counseling, I was sometimes consulted by people burdened with a sense of guilt about feeling unable to forgive an evil done to them. I learned to ask, "How would this whole sad story be different if you were approached by the person who has hurt you, with tears in his or her eyes, and with remorse written all over his or her face? What difference would it make to you if he or she pleaded with you to somehow find it in your heart to forgive the great wickedness you have suffered at his or her hand? Would you think differently about forgiving this person if he or she actually got down on bended knee in front of you, and with great sobbing and weeping, begged you for forgiveness?"

Forgiving someone "as the Lord has forgiven you" is this second species of forgiveness. This forgiveness, by definition, is granted <u>conditionally</u> on the guilty person's confession and repentance.

Armed with these two quite different practices of forgiveness, and willing to use either of them, as appropriate, the Lord's people will not be "overcome by evil, but [will] overcome evil with good."

Piece #22:   BORN IN A COFFEE SHOP

What if through a set of unusual circumstances, a healthy baby was born in a well-established coffee shop? And what if the happy parents were so thrilled about the whole experience that they bought that coffee shop, and built themselves a lovely apartment on the second floor. There, they could raise their child, and very conveniently, their commute to work would be one flight of stairs.

Perhaps the conclusion is not obvious. But it seems to me that that baby, when quite grown up, would have absolutely no excuse for not knowing that there *is* such a thing as coffee. Someone might ask, how could it ever happen that such a person would be unaware of the fact of coffee's existence? It does seem self-evident that such a privileged person would not only be aware of the existence of coffee, but highly informed about the various glories of our modern civilization's most popular, legal, addictive psychotropic beverage.

The apostle Paul in his letter to the Romans makes a similar point in regard to every person in this world being born and raised on earth. He wrote, "… what can be known about God is <u>plain</u> to them, because God has <u>shown</u> it to them. For <u>his invisible attributes</u>, namely, <u>his eternal power and divine nature</u>, have been <u>clearly perceived,</u> ever since the creation of the world, in the things that have been made. So they are without excuse" [Romans 1:19,20].

Personally, as one of many earth-born, earth-raised human beings, I would like to state that I see, here again, that the apostle is speaking truth. This world *is* a remarkable place, with its breathtaking sunrises, awe-inspiring sunsets, majestic mountains, and its billions of unique snowflakes. And also, its 40,000-kilometre per year migrating Arctic Terns. And its complex and precise atmosphere, in which we humans "live and breathe and have our being." And, of course, added to all those wonders, there is also really good coffee to drink. This world being what it is—and so obviously marvelous—we who have always lived here have no excuse for denying that God exists, or denying that we, whose existence depends entirely on the continued existence of this world, are entirely dependent upon him. Dependent upon him, and very much indebted to him.

AFTERWORD

I explained in the Introduction how I came to believe that a teacher is being especially helpful when he states his own opinion on a subject, and then explains why he thinks that. Of course, in an actual classroom, such a teacher can be questioned—and almost certainly likes to be. I know that in my years of pastoral teaching, I always appreciated questions.

This book is comprised of 66 of my highly opinionated views. The equivalent of a "Q & A" session is the page on the book's website entitled "Ask the Author." It can be found at <u>444book.com</u>. I would love to try to answer your questions!

ACKNOWLEDGEMENTS
from the author

Here I express my very heartfelt thanks to Ray Majoran, Derek McLachlin and Jessica Wilkins, who kindly took the time to edit "4:44." Their whole-hearted, eagle-eyed attention to every word and every sentence of this book, and their personal opinions and suggestions regarding the comprehensibility and practical value of each Bit and each Piece were a great help to me in seeking to make this book worth a reader's time and effort to read. Nonetheless, blame for any remaining typographical errors and other nasty imperfections is, tragically, mine alone.

ABOUT "GLORY IN THE FACE"
by the author

An account of my adult life can perhaps best be made by dividing it in two: the healthy part and the non-healthy part. Happily for me, the healthy part was about three decades in length; many more years than the non-healthy part.

I was just turning 30 when the first part began, and I began pastoring West London Alliance Church in London, Ontario. That was 1984. Although the church and I both went through a number of changes over those years, there was a happy sameness both to my work, and my sense of privilege to be busy with it. Then, at the age of 57, I began to transition to Part Two, which officially began in 2015 when I resigned from all active pastoral duties.

Part Two, which obviously continues to this day, has been primarily comprised of doctor's appointments and other medical things-to-do, reading, writing, chatting and drinking coffee with one of my very good friends, and lying around the house in a state of general exhaustion.

Glory in the Face is my account of experiences in both parts of my life by which I learned how to be strong enough in the Lord to face challenges of many sorts. What I have learned, and have tried to explain in the book, is how that strength is received through God's gift of the peace that can guard our hearts and minds from despair, and God's gift of joy which comes from his daily presence in our lives, and which strengthens us to face anything.

Endorsements of GLORY IN THE FACE

Rev. Sunder Krishnan served as the Preaching Pastor of Rexdale Alliance Church (in Toronto), from 1980-2016, and was its Senior Pastor since 1996. He is the author of several books, including *The Conquest of Inner Space: Finding Peace in a Chaotic World, Loving God with All You've Got, Catching the Wind of the Spirit,* and *Hijacked by Glory: From the Pew to the Nations.*

> *"Finding the strength to face anything"!* What qualifies someone to write a book that accomplishes such a formidable objective. For starters, *a command of the English language* so that the reading itself would be a pleasure. Secondly, *a well developed, truly biblical theology* since the source of the strength is God himself. Thirdly, *wisdom to apply the knowledge of God's character and ways* to the point where the proverbial rubber meets the road in the life of the reader. Fourthly and perhaps most importantly, *finding that very strength* to handle prolonged personal suffering without loss of faith and with grace. In my friend Mike Wilkins, these four strands have converged to produce the book that you now hold in your hands. It will remain one of my most treasured possessions, celebrating as it does, a blessed friendship that has lasted 33 years at the time of writing."

Endorsements of GLORY IN THE FACE

Dr. Bruce W. Longenecker is Professor of Early Christianity and the Melton Chair of Religion at Baylor University (Texas). He is the author of a number of books, including *The Lost Letters of Pergamum* (Baker Academic), *The Cross before Constantine: The Early Life of a Christian Symbol* (Fortress Press) and *The Crosses of Pompeii: Jesus-Devotion in a Vesuvian Town*.

> "For more than four decades, Mike Wilkins has blessed many with his faithful, creative, engaging, and practical expositions of Scripture. His challenging and inspiring reflections in this book are no exception. Light-heartedly interspersing poignant musings on his own life (and his recent "fall from health") with skilled and masterful meditations on Scripture, Wilkins insightfully probes the deep theological soils of one of the apostle Paul's richest letters (2 Corinthians).

Dr. Carolyn Weber is an award-winning author, speaker and professor. Her books include *Surprised by Oxford* (HarperCollins) and *Holy is the Day* (IVP).

> "With wit, humour, intelligence and wisdom, Wilkins shares his deep love for God with a poignancy that comes from a life lived earnestly to the glory of God. He does this with an illuminating nod to other spiritual thinkers who have helped him on this journey. Whether in joy or grief, contentedness or suffering, Wilkins' words remind us that God's glory permeates our broken world with intimations of hope for the restored one. In seeking God's face, we face nothing, not even death, alone. And in the seeking, nothing, not even death, is in vain."

ABOUT THE AUTHOR

Mike Wilkins was born in 1954 in Kingston, Ontario, but did most of his growing up 50 miles along the St. Lawrence River in the pretty little city of Brockville. In 1973, Mike met his future wife, Debbie Street, when they were both 18 years old. Four years later, in four short weeks, he and Deb graduated from Queen's University and married each other, and Mike started a full-time job at a publisher of children's books.

In 1984, with two young kids—and hopes of a third one some day—Mike and Deb moved to London, Ontario, where Mike became the pastor of West London Alliance Church. For the many years he continued that ministry, Deb was a stay-at-home mom for Jessica, Ben and Joanna, then also their homeschool teacher, and then an employee of Compassion Canada, where (at the time of this writing) she still works happily.

While he was a healthy adult, Mike's hobbies—in addition to child-raising—were long-distance running, canoe-tripping, reading (and re-reading) old books, and writing and directing plays and musicals. Then, in 2013, he was diagnosed with metastatic colorectal cancer, which (to the time of this writing) continues to change almost all of the details of his daily life.

Mike is also the author of *Glory in the Face ~ the face of Christ and the strength to face anything* (www.gloryintheface.com), and the children's novel *Island Family,* a "pseudo-autobiographical" novel for ages 7 to 11 (www.islandfamily.ca).

CPSIA information can be obtained
at www.ICGtesting.com
Printed in the USA
LVHW08s0034310718
585378LV00001B/135/P